THE SUPERTEAM SOLUTION

DEDICATED TO

All aspiring Superteams

'There's no use trying', said Alice, 'one can't believe impossible things.'

'I daresay you haven't had much practice', said the Queen, 'when I was your age, I always did it for half an hour a day. Why, sometimes, I've believed as many as six impossible things before breakfast'

Lewis Carroll, Through the Looking Glass

'The only way to discover the limits of the possible is to go beyond them into the impossible'

Clark's Credo

THE SUPERTEAM SOLUTION

Successful Teamworking in Organisations

Colin Hastings, Peter Bixby,
and
Rani Chaudhry-Lawton

University Associates, Inc.
8517 Production Avenue
San Diego, California 92121

Original paperbound edition
(*Superteams: A Blueprint for Organisational Success*)
published by:

William Collins Sons & Co. Ltd.
8 Grafton Street
London, England
W1X 3LA

Contents

Preface

This book is about teams in organisations. It's about new ways of using old teams and about new ways of using new kinds of teams. But more than that, it's about what it takes to create teams that perform outstandingly well — we call them Superteams. It's also about how our organisations, be they public or private sector, service or manufacturing, need to harness the magic of high performing teams in new and innovative ways to help them respond to new challenges that at times may appear to verge on the impossible. In order to achieve this, we argue, Superteams need to operate within enlightened organisations which provide them with purpose, support and opportunity. In short, we argue the need for a partnership between team and organisation.

We ourselves are a small team; part of a larger group of consultants and developers who spend much of their time understanding teams by working with them. We draw much of our inspiration and excitement from our clients – people like yourself who are leaders or members of a variety of teams in organisations. We owe them a lot because they have taught us a lot. For what you read in this book is not the product of academic research (although our academic training has certainly helped us to analyse and digest what we see) but a distillation of what we and others have found to be useful in practice.

To protect the confidentiality of our clients, we have either used pseudonyms or left the source of examples deliberately vague. In some cases, too, we have had to exercise a degree of journalistic licence in order to make our point without running the risk of identifying a particular person or organisation. Direct references to people or organisations are therefore all from published sources.

For the reader's benefit, the first part of the book ('The Genesis of Superteams') summarises our arguments. Chapter 1 outlines some of the new challenges that modern organisations will have to face and why Superteams have a central contribution to make in meeting them. Chapter 2 explains what we mean by Superteams and gives a simple explanation of the Ashridge Team-Working Approach, the framework that we use to develop team performance. Chapter 3 outlines a range of new ways in which teamworking can be promoted in organisations. It is a quick guide to using Superteams, and suggests a crucial role for senior people in creating the right conditions for Superteams to be successful.

For those with more time or a deeper interest, Part Two ('The Hallmark of Superteams') goes on to develop the themes of Chapter 2 further. The eight elements of The Ashridge Team-Working Approach are expanded in detail in Chapters 4 to 11, each chapter ending with a number of short, practical suggestions for improving team effectiveness. Part Three ('Teamworking Projects') provides a series of succinct examples illustrating the range of innovative approaches that some organisations are already adopting to anticipate and solve pressing new problems through the active promotion of teams and teamworking. The final section, 'Some Guidelines for Success', encapsulates our own, and other people's, experience of what to do and what not to do when promoting teamwork in organisations. In particular the guidelines try to indicate what organisations of the future can start doing now to improve their performance through teamworking.

That then is what we offer. We hope you enjoy reading it as much as we have enjoyed researching and writing it.

Colin Hastings
Peter Bixby
Rani Chaudhry-Lawton

Acknowledgements

We should like to extend our warmest thanks to an invisible team —
all those people in the background who in one way or another,
wittingly or unwittingly, have helped us to bring this book to fruition.

The book was conceived as a result of work that we have been doing
together over the last three years at Ashridge Management College.
Without the stimulus, the opportunity and the resources that
Ashridge has provided, the book would never have happened. Our
colleague David Pearce has been closely involved with the development of the Ashridge Teamworking Approach from its inception and
his contribution and support have never flagged. In the early stages
Mona Hipwell and Kevin Barham too made particularly valuable
contributions.

During the hectic four weeks when we were writing the book, we
had especially wonderful help from Carolyn Elliott our secretary and
co-ordinator. She is truly a key person in our team — her speed and
skill on the word processor have contributed enormously as has her
calm, cheerful and persistent approach to the whole task. We should
also particularly like to thank our colleague Michael Geddes, who
kindly contributed the case study in Chapter 15. Also deserving of
special mention are the Ashridge library staff who were tireless in
searching for information, and Ken Walker, the college's Visual Aids
Designer, who drew our diagram. We must also acknowledge our debt

to the *Financial Times* for providing frequent stimulus and lines of investigation.

It is insuperably difficult, having immersed ourselves in the subject of teamwork in organisations now for several years, to identify all those people who have contributed to the development of our ideas. We apologise to those who see some of themselves between these pages and whom we have not acknowledged. We can only assure you that we value and appreciate the fact that many other people's thoughts have contributed to our own and that any forgetfulness or omission on our part is in no way deliberate.

If writing a book is a bit like bearing a child, our editor at Gower, Malcolm Stern, has been both consultant gynaecologist and midwife! He has given us a great deal of freedom to create what we wanted, for which we are grateful. However, his willingness to help and guide and give generously of his experience has, we believe, kept us firmly on track. For us, it has been a most fruitful relationship.

Finally, we come to our families. All three of our spouses probably feel that they have been living with this book for four years rather than four weeks. Indeed each of them has contributed ideas in his or her own professional right. Colin's two children, aged seven and five, when asked to brainstorm titles, contributed by suggesting 'Flying Kipper Teams' for the front cover, and were phlegmatic about having the idea rejected by the publisher. But all of them have contributed most by supporting us while our time and affection was temporarily diverted to the book. So, to Helen, Nicholas, Matthew, Richard and Ann, our love and very special thanks.

C H
P B
R C-L

PART ONE
The Genesis of Superteams

1 The demands of the future

It is a bright spring morning and the place is Baltimore, USA. John Young, President and Chief Executive Officer of Hewlett Packard has just delivered a powerful opening speech to the Annual Congress of the American Society for Quality Control. He has stressed that what he calls conformance assurance, or working to basic technical standards, while essential, is not a good enough standard of performance any longer for organisations that want to survive in the future.

It is a cool summer morning and the place is Coventry, England. Jim Randle, Engineering Director of Jaguar Cars, is being interviewed by the editor of a prestigious motor magazine about one of the company's much heralded new models. 'The current car has already put many a hurdle in the path of the new design' he explains 'It's not as if we were building a new car to improve on a bad one. We're putting as much effort as ever into improving the present range, and people still tell us they're among the world's best cars. But this means our goals for the new model keep shifting. The old car's standards get harder to exceed. It can make life very complicated.'

Jim Randle, like John Young, is living in a world where the best is no longer good enough. John Young in his speech suggests that a crucial element in achieving higher levels of performance is the creation of organisational environments which encourage teamwork.

We share that belief and this book is our contribution to making it happen.

Before looking at teams and teamworking in detail, we want to take a look at some of the things that are happening to modern organisations. For we believe that the reason why teamworking is coming to the fore so strongly is that it offers organisations a means for responding positively to the demands for quantum leaps in performance that they face.

THE PRESSURE TO PERFORM

For most large organisations, the events of the last decade have imposed huge demands to re-think what they do and how they do it. For some, the main thrust of their strategy for survival lay in the search for more efficient approaches. In its most visible form this has meant slimming down the labour force, tightening up financial controls by trimming costs and investment in technological solutions, such as computers and robots.

This response is an attractive one. It is based on analysis, rationality and objectivity. It preserves a model of organisational life which is familiar. It is also clearly necessary in the drive to gain and maintain competitive advantage or to use scarce resources wisely. But this form of drive towards increased efficiency is potentially damaging if pursued in isolation, since a lean organisation is not necessarily a fit one. A state of organisational health is achieved not simply by shedding the fat, but through a process of questioning whether what remains is being used in the best way.

Yet achieving fitness to complement leanness is not so easy. Where the drive for leanness can be and often is stimulated by some form of threat such as reduced market share, economic downturn or reduced Government funding, the pursuit of fitness arises more from dissatisfaction with what is and the determination to find better ways of doing things.

For instance, cost efficiency and economies of scale alone are not enough to explain how Daimler–Benz has become the World's leading manufacturer of medium and heavy trucks. It's as much due to an obsession with customer service, flexibility in being able to offer twelve hundred different models of truck with twenty-two thousand special variations, and tenaciousness in being able to adapt to continuously changing circumstances.

The West's biggest car manufacturers are belatedly realising that their average new model development programme of about seven years is not good enough even to be able to respond to market changes. The problem however is even more acute when it emerges that the average Japanese programme takes about three years. In the high technology, consumer, service and fashion related industries, product life cycles are even shorter, rapid planned obsolence being part of the strategy for staying at the leading edge of competitiveness. The downside of course is that failure to bring a reliable product or service onto the market even by a matter of weeks, can be disastrous.

A PROBLEM OF LIFESTYLE

Organisations can be certain of only one thing, and that is that life is increasingly uncertain. For commercial organisations these uncertainties come from intense global competition, rapidly changing markets and shifting technologies. For non-commercial organisations tighter Government spending, political fluidity and closer scrutiny by a more informed and demanding public pose challenges. For all organisations, the costs of research and development and the changing expectations and aspirations of employees compound the conflicting and changing priorities that they are trying to juggle.

Uncertainty therefore is now normal. So is the complexity of the problems that it brings. These are the new realities. Many organisations have grown fat and bureaucratic on past stability and predictability. And they find, often painfully, that slimming down merely leaves them weak and vulnerable. Too often the slimming process only treats the symptoms and not the causes of the problem. We find not so much a weight problem as a lifestyle problem.

How then does an organisation develop and maintain a state of health which will drive it towards success? The answer lies in appreciating the heavy investment which exists in the conventional wisdom of organisational life. Given that the model upon which the majority of our organisations are formed has its origins in the Industrial Revolution, custom and practice provide some powerful precedents which it is not easy to discard. This is especially so when the model has proved its value and indeed continues to do so. It is ideally suited to stable, predictable conditions and to handling routine activities. Many organisations however are now faced with complexity and change as a way of life and the certainty that continued success can only come from rapid adaptation.

For some organisations, the traditional route will continue to serve well. For increasing numbers it will not. The need for faster response times, to initiate actions rather than merely respond to challenges from the market place, from competitors, from technological advances and from social, political and economic change, all conspire to increase the likelihood that any organisation which wants substantially to improve its performance levels will need to seek new ways of doing so.

In coming to terms with these changes, the more successful organisations are prepared to examine the very way they organise, the way they see their customers, the way they change and the way that they go about getting the best out of their people. Challenging and changing these underlying values and assumptions is the first step in developing the fitness needed to survive in, and thrive on the demands of, the future.

ALTERNATIVE FUTURES

So what are the alternatives? What kinds of organisation are needed to produce outstanding performance under conditions of constant change and uncertainty?

Some of the answers are already around us. The Oxford Instrument Group is a World leader in cryogenics and nuclear magnetic resonance. It started off with one business and over the last decade has spawned several more. Each new business has been built round an individual or small team who had an idea for a new product. Each was given two years to prove its viability, with lots of support but little interference from the Board. The success of this strategy has recently led to a successful flotation of the group on the stock market. Johnson and Johnson in the USA has taken a similar approach even further with the result that it now has literally hundreds of highly decentralised divisions run by committed 'product champions'.

Goldman, Sachs and Co. is one of the most successful Wall Street investment firms because of its distinct corporate culture. This culture encompasses teamwork and the lack of star system, whereby no one person takes credit for a success. The client always comes first, even if it hurts Goldman's relationship with other Wall Street firms. The firm practices loose management combined with tight controls, whereby operational rigidity is balanced with freedom in day-to-day decision making and entrepreneurship and innovation are strongly encouraged.

GMW is a small company which specialises in developing special equipment to enable architects to design buildings by computer. Individuals who have ideas for any improvements to the company's products, services or organisation are encouraged to form 'bubbles'. A bubble consists of a few people interested in pursuing the idea. Once the bubble is given the go ahead, people in it are paid extra for working in it but are expected to do their everyday jobs as well. The management accepts that most bubbles will probably burst. But sufficient new ideas, innovations and motivation come out of them to make the gains far outweigh the losses. 3M in the USA encourages something similar – they call them 'skunk works' — small groups taking an idea, doing some quick experimentation to test its feasibility with users, taking it forward if it looks to have potential, but dropping it quickly if it shows no promise. British Airways has a different variant: Customer First Teams investigating ways in which the airline's service and services can be improved.

SRI International is a world renowned research and consultancy organisation with a very loosely knit organisation. It is divided into very small units or cells each of which has to pay its own way. The successful ones get more of the distributed profits than the less successful ones. The result as one of their consultants put it 'is that bits die off when they can't support themselves'. But the organisation is amoeba-like — it re-forms round individuals whose proposals are accepted and then divides in a very fluid way.

A new word has entered management jargon to describe some of these happenings. Gifford Pinchot III has coined the word 'intrapreneurial' to denote individuals or small teams operating in an entrepreneurial fashion within organisations for the benefit of themselves and of the organisation. British Aerospace, who build the famous Harrier Jump Jet, from time to time create Tiger Teams. These are troubleshooting groups put together at short notice and very short periods of time to sort out difficult problems. One such problem occurred soon after the delivery of a batch of planes to a foreign air force. The Tiger Team, five hand picked specialists, was on the spot within twenty-four hours. The problem was solved completely within three days.

The aerospace business in particular has been a world leader in the formation of cross-national joint ventures. Recently an important step forward was taken by European governments in setting up the Eureka project, a systematic programme designed to bring together European companies in research and development of high technology products for commercial application. Though fraught with difficulties, the formation of these cross-national teams is the only way to fund the enormous costs of such developments. An ebullient French spokesman announcing the end of tortuous negotiations between different governments was quoted in *Time* magazine as saying, 'The mayonnaise is beginning to gel'; in other words the potential to be achieved from co-operative team working across frontiers is beginning to outweight the vested interests of individual countries.

A pattern emerges from all these examples which demonstrate the new increasingly important roles that teams and teamworking are playing.

All these examples are from organisations that are leading the way in searching out schemes for being and staying adaptable. They all create 'turned on' teams by devolving large amounts of authority and responsibility to these teams to create a destiny within a broader framework of mission and support provided by the organisation. They use involvement in teams as a way of releasing as yet untapped talent within the organisation. With their accent on high performance they make these teams and the individuals within them accountable for the pursuit of organisational goals. They are all aware of the huge leap in achievement that can come from really outstanding teams, and they all strive to create an organisational environment which from the highest to the lowest level promotes and supports teamwork, innovation and change.

SUPERTEAMS

To us there seem to be two main threads. The first of these is the idea of the high performing team which produces quite outstanding achievements. We call these Superteams. Says Tom Peters, co-author of the best seller *In search of excellence*, 'the amount of performance improvement that is possible from these turned on teams is not small — it is enormous'. The second is the idea that there are many new ways of using teams emerging and that somewhere in these new teamworking strategies are some answers for organisations which want to face the future now.

The next two chapters summarise how this is being done in practice.

2 The Superteam vision

We must confess that we have not as yet seen or worked with a Superteam. The reason for this is that the Superteam concept is an ideal, a target, something to be striven for. That is why we call it the Superteam vision, because although unlikely to be achieved in its entirety, we believe it provides an exciting model to which any team can aspire.

What we have done is to piece together all the evidence that we can find, from our own and other people's work, in order to put together a comprehensive picture of what it is that makes some teams outstanding in comparison with others. We believe that this picture draws out and summarises the best practice from the best of modern teams.

What we are certain of is that the vast majority of teams grossly underperform. What we are also clear about is that high levels of success in teams are not down to the good fortune of being around at the right time. Superteams' successes happen because they are made to happen and because the team understands how to make them happen. We have created the Superteam Vision in order to help many more teams make it happen.

Many teams, at least initially, seem to find it very difficult indeed to think about their performance in any systematic way or to analyse what factors help and hinder their achievements. That is why we have codified the Superteam Vision in a simple, structured form which we refer to as The Ashridge Team-Working Approach. This provides a number of practical tools that team leaders and team members can use to work at enhancing their own and their teams' performance.

We believe that the approach is unique in a number of ways. First it starts by looking at *performance*. Furthermore it does not content itself with just acceptable performance because in every aspect of their functioning Superteams strive for outstanding performance. It is this one characteristic above all else that distinguishes Superteams from ordinary teams. The approach is therefore about quality in all its aspects, and in particular defines quality from the customers or clients point of view, for it is these expectations that the team is there to satisfy, whatever the type of team.

Secondly, the approach recognises that teams are not independent: they live within organisations and a considerable element in their success lies in their management of resources outside the team. We felt that too often in the past, teams have been developed independently of the organisation which is their lifeblood. What characterises our approach to working with teams therefore is that we spend time bringing together and working with those from both inside and outside the team.

THE QUALITIES OF SUPERTEAMS

The secrets that make Superteams so successful are complex and varied. These teams weave together a rich fabric of competences, experience, attitudes and values which create a tightly woven, integrated cloth suitable for many purposes. Superteams need to be seen as whole entities, in the round, for each of their admirable attributes both contributes to and feeds off the others.

Describing these qualities only briefly is therefore a difficult task and carries all the risks of conveying only a partial picture. But we want to give busy readers at least the flavours of the Superteam in these early chapters as well as to tempt them to explore the Superteam Vision more deeply in Part Two.

What follows therefore is a series of small tasters which, between them, summarise the qualities of Superteams.

- Superteams are persistent and obsessive in the pursuit of their goals, but creatively flexible in their strategies for getting there. They are continuously returning to the question, 'What are we trying to achieve?'

- Superteams confront people or situations which lie in their path. They are tenacious and inventive in their efforts to remove all obstacles.

- Superteams are committed to quality in performance and all aspects of teamworking. They have very high expectations of themselves and of others.

- Superteams display significant understanding of the strategy and philosophy of their parent organisation or that part of it which is important to their success.

- Superteams are inspired by a vision of what they are trying to achieve. This provides a strong sense of purpose and direction. They also have a realistic strategy for turning the vision into reality.

- Superteams actively build formal and informal networks which include people who matter to them and who can help them.

- Superteams make themselves visible and accessible to others. They communicate strongly what they stand for, but they welcome advice and comments from outside.

- Superteams are driven by success. They exude the energy, excitement and commitment that being successful releases. They also thrive on the recognition that success brings.

- Superteams are action-oriented. They respond quickly and positively to problems and opportunities and are optimistic even when the going gets tough. But above all they don't wait for things to happen to them. They go out and make things happen: things happen.

- Superteams are committed to the success of their parent organisation. They thrive in an open culture where responsibility and authority is delegated to them to produce agreed results.

- Superteams have a significant influence on the parent organisation. The power to influence is not based on formal authority but on the teams' credibility. Team and organisation feed off and learn from each other.

- Superteams work best with principles and guidelines as procedures rather than rules. In this way they preserve one of their key qualities — flexibility.

- Superteams distinguish the important from the urgent, and while valuing change and flexibility will make routine those activities which can be dealt with most effectively in that way.

- Superteams value leaders who maintain the teams' direction, energy and commitment. They expect the leader, with their help, to fight for support and resources from key figures within the parent organisation.

- Superteams are able to sustain communication and momentum as well when they are working apart as when they are working together.

- Superteams pride themselves on being creative and innovative and on being prepared to take legitimate risks in order to achieve significant gains.

- Superteams understand why they are successful but are never satisfied with that. They are constantly looking for ways to 'do things better'.

- Superteams value people for their knowledge, competence and contributions rather than for status and position.

- Superteams will always try to work *with* others rather than working for or against others.

- Superteams sometimes seem arrogant — and this can be the cause of their downfall!

THE ASHRIDGE TEAM-WORKING APPROACH

While the qualities that we have outlined above capture the essence of the Superteam Vision, the more practical minded will want to know what Superteams actually do to bring it about. This is the purpose of the Ashridge Team-Working Approach.

Once again, we are providing a summary to give the flavour of the approach. The summary can also be used as a convenient checklist. Each of the eight elements is covered in detail in the chapters that make up Part Two of the book.

1. Negotiating success criteria

Who specifies success — important roles outside the team that define the teams' success criteria.

Dimensions of success — how to describe outstanding performance.

Contracting — the process by which common understanding about requirements and expectations is reached.

The lure of success — the driving force behind Superteams is the motivation that comes from being successful.

2. Managing the outside

The invisible team — important roles outside the team that are crucial to its success.

Image — how the teams' credibility and competence is seen by outsiders.

Building connections — identifying a network of people who can help.

Preparing the ground — spending time developing key relationships.

Mobilising resources — getting what the team needs when it's wanted.

Insiders and outsiders — some dangers to watch for.

3. Planning the what

Challenging mediocrity — attitudes to planning affect a teams' ability to perform outstandingly.

Making enemies out of friends — how planners can alienate themselves from team members — and what to do about it.

Planning the known — the Superteam approach to planning the predictable.

Planning the unknown — the Superteam approach to planning under conditions of uncertainty.

Milestones not millstones — the importance to members' motivation of achieving regular progress and success.

4. Planning the how

Developing ground rules for success — 'the way we do things round here'

Managing the outside — deciding how the team is to conduct itself with outsiders.

Driving it forward — where does the energy come from and how is it sustained?

Binding it together — or better perhaps 'how to stop it all falling apart'

Changing the rules — as the situation changes and develops, so too might the rules.

5. Leading the team

Looking forwards — providing direction and creating an environment that stimulates high performance.

Managing team members performance — defining, monitoring and rewarding outstanding performance.

Looking inwards — constantly analysing how the team is working and how it can be improved.

Looking outwards — ensuring a two-way flow of information, resources and support between the team and outsiders.

6. Membership

Beliefs about leaders — what it takes to be able to support the leader.

Beliefs about followership — active rather than passive followership is most helpful to the team.

Beliefs about specialists — seeing other specialisms as a help and not a hindrance.

Beliefs about roles — being clear about what needs to be fixed and what needs to be flexible.

Beliefs about co-operation — preserving the benefits of individualism and competitiveness without jeopardising cooperation.

Beliefs about performance — the difference between those team members who produce outstanding as opposed to mediocre results.

7. The team together

Why are we coming together — an examination of the many different purposes served by coming together.

How to work well together — some of the basic disciplines that make meetings go well.

Conflict — some strategies and tactics for resolving differences.

Is there life after meetings — when the talking must stop and the action must begin.

8. The team apart

Great expectations — all team members are expected to deliver what they said, when they said

Holding on and letting go — keeping the important objectives to the fore while trusting team members to manage their own priorities and distractions.

Maintaining commitment and momentum — keeping up the pressure

Active communications — taking positive steps to stay in touch and spot problems early.

These then are the qualities, strategies and skills of the Superteam. In the next chapter we suggest that new ways of developing and using Superteams are already providing organisations with some powerful means of meeting the demands of the future.

3 Success through Superteams

In Chapter 1, we showed briefly how a whole new range of team-working strategies and opportunities was evolving as organisations grappled with the demands of the future. Some organisations are experimenting boldly and learning fast from their successes and failures. Others are more tentative.

Peter Drucker, in the foreword to his book *The Age of Discontinuity* observes:

> It [the book] does not ask: 'What will tomorrow look like?' It asks instead: 'What do we have to tackle today to make tomorrow happen?'

This book crystallises some of the things that are already taking place to make tomorrow happen. If a crucial part of the organisational future lies in radical new uses of teamworking, then the future is here now and Superteams are part of it. But the range of possible teamwork strategies is not yet entirely clear, nor can we yet be certain what conditions are necessary for them to be successful.

This chapter is our contribution to clarifying these issues. In the following section, 'Seven Superteam strategies', we briefly outline seven different approaches to developing and using the power of teams and teamwork in your organisation.

In the last section of this chapter, 'Creating the conditions for success', we summarise briefly the two main contributions that we believe senior management of organisations can make to ensuring that their experiments with the new teamworking strategies are successful.

SEVEN SUPERTEAM STRATEGIES

1 Strategy development and implementation

> 'Wisdom comes not from knowing the answers but in realising how many questions remain' *Richard Berendzen*

As organisations become more complex, it becomes increasingly difficult for any top team in an organisation to grasp all the factors that need to be taken into account in developing and implementing strategy. That is why more and more of them are involving greater numbers of people in contributing to the process. It is a way of drawing more widely on the talents available in the organisation as well as securing greater commitment to the results.

Under these circumstances, cross-departmental teams, which bring together people of diverse experience and expertise, have a particularly relevant role to play, both in the formulation of strategy and in implementing it within the organisation. The very process of working in teams such as this can, if well managed, also have a very marked impact on the teamworking climate within the organisation.

2 Restructuring

> 'We trained very hard, but it seemed that every time we were beginning to form up into teams, we would be reorganised. I was to learn later in life that we tended to react to any new situation by reorganising, and a wonderful method it can be for creating the illusion of progress, while producing confusion, inefficiency and demoralisation' *Petronius, AD 66*

. . an organisation chart is not a company, nor a new strategy, an automatic answer to corporate grief. We all know this; but like as not, when trouble lurks, we call for a new strategy and probably reorganise. And when we reorganise, we usually stop at rearranging the boxes on the chart. The odds are high that nothing much will change. We will have chaos, even useful chaos for a while, but eventually the old culture will prevail. Old habit patterns persist.'

Peters and Waterman, AD 1982

Looking at the two quotations above, it seems that nothing much changes in organisations, especially when it comes to reorganisations!

But the frequent cynicism and disillusion about reorganisation and its consequences (or lack of them) need not be that way. There is now a growing body of understanding about how reorganisations can be brought about more skilfully and in such a way as to ensure achievement of the hard criteria of improved productivity, quality or service, as well as of the soft criteria of people's commitment. Organisations cannot afford to allow changes to be disruptive and demotivating. The aim must be to ensure that these changes are implanted, stabilised and come 'on-line' quickly and with full commitment.

Being successful at reorganising becomes even more difficult when part of the purpose, as say in a decentralisation process, is also to change attitudes and responsibilities. In this case, people are suddenly expected to be far more autonomous, and to manage their own affairs more, perhaps after years of reacting to central direction.

Reorganisation and restructuring therefore, seldom have one simple objective; there are many layers of purpose. And in order to achieve all these, and achieve them speedily without too many adverse consequences, requires a sufficient investment of managerial time and money. This investment can give excellent returns if channelled into developing the new teams created by the restructuring in order for them to accept the responsibility and find the commitment to make that restructuring work in practice.

3 Joint ventures and mergers

'Joint-venture research is like flirtation — you never know how far it will go'

George Van Houten:
board member for research, Philips

There is little doubt that mergers and joint ventures are on the increase, not only within but across national borders. Stories of success and failure are mixed — some successes such as Saab–Lancia and AT and T–Olivetti have been well publicised as have some big failures such as Dunlop–Pirelli and Agfa–Gevaert. These are the large and dramatic examples which are the tip of the iceberg that hides a host of smaller cooperative ventures between different people and organisations that are sprouting widely.

How then can organisations contemplating such moves guarantee success — for the cost of failure is high. Mergers and joint ventures stand or fall on their ability to get people working well together. The object must be to create integrated teams from the two partners that are able to achieve more than either partner could individually. Often that involves bringing together two or more different technologies and systems. But most difficult of all, it involves mixing two different organisational cultures, two different sets of attitudes and values about what makes a good organisation. One rueful executive who had experienced a failed joint venture commented, 'it was like putting together oil and vinegar; we just couldn't get it to mix'. If the recipe also includes differences in national cultures and economic systems, the would be joint-venture chef's problems are compounded. However, the potential payoffs are enormous in creating high-performing joint venture or merger teams.

4 Project teams within organisations

'To: Father Noah

From: The Lord

Subject: Request for time extension for Project Ark.

Unfortunately, Project Ark lies on the critical path of Project Deluge.

REQUEST DENIED

The Lord'

Mike Berger, *If Noah built the Ark today*

Modern organisations are becoming increasingly schizophrenic. They have two main characters and that, we believe, is a thoroughly good thing! Let us explain. On the one hand the organisation has a structure and people devoted to managing day to day routine activities; we might call this its operational character. On the other hand the same people, but brought together from different parts of the structure, are working on non-routine activities — usually one-off projects or work to do with the development and change of the organisation, its technology or systems; we might call this its project character. British Telecom International for instance, which manages all the UK's international telecommunications, often have individuals in many different locations and departments working on the same in-company project. In recent years they have begun to bring these teams together on a regular basis (making the invisible team visible) so that they can build a real team and work out more systematically how they are going to perform effectively.

A big European pharmaceutical company has one hundred and forty 'temporary task groups' in its Research and Development laboratory in Germany alone. They work on a wide range of products and issues. 'I've counted a number of key people who are involved in as many as twelve of these groups', says Ingrid Schwartz the management development manager. 'All our people need to have a common teamworking philosophy. There's no time to invent new rules for each team. They need to work effectively from the start. The problem is how do I do it.'

There is a huge range of different kinds of project within organisations that can be well handled by project or by temporary task groups. Sometimes they justify full time leaders and members but often they are part time activities to be fitted round other responsibilities. Getting a team to work effectively under these circumstances is a challenge to all concerned.

Amongst the wide range of tasks that these teams can undertake, we have found the following to be the most common (not in any special order)

Co-ordinating an office move
Introducing a new computer or administrative system
Co-ordinating a change of company name
Preparing a stand for a trade exhibition
New product development and launch
Installing new capital equipment
Building and equipping new premises
Takeover/Merger feasibility study and implementation
Installing a new telephone system

---

5 Teamworking across departments

'Our organisation is divided up into watertight compartments — just like the Titanic!'   *European Editor, international magazine*

Hospital administrators know only too well how many different specialisms contribute to patient care. 'The basic trouble here' said one 'is that they don't communicate with each other with the result that we seem to lurch from one panic to the next. If only they'd get together more often and work out the problems together we'd save a lot of time, energy and aggravation. 'But I don't know how to get them to do that.'

But the problem is of course not only one that faces hospital administrators. 'There are four people who should be the corner-stones of my factory' said James Young. James is production director of a factory making knitwear, where the mix is always changing according to fashion and season. 'The trouble is' he continued, 'that the structure doesn't make them look like a team but they have to be'. The four people that he is referring to are the market forecaster, the production planner, the raw materials buyer and the distribution manager. 'One cannot sneeze without the others being affected. And if they don't get it right, and don't work closely together, then we have major problems. Each of them needs to be very different but what each must have is a teamwork-ing mentality'. . . .

The common factor in these two situations is the need for cooperation and teamworking across departments. These different departments often only meet formally at the leader level. But on a day-to-day basis it is cooperation at the member level that counts. There are always members in different departments who have common interests and need to see themselves as a team. We call these invisible teams because the formal structure seldom reveals them.

In a slightly different way, some organisations are constantly bringing together specialists from different departments to do specific projects. 'The members of our audit teams are constantly changing as an audit progresses' said a senior partner in an international accountancy firm. 'What we need is a pool of people who can slot quickly in and out of teams.' And that perhaps is the crux of the matter. How can organisations develop pools of specialists in different departments who can work well across departmental boundaries? This will be a crucial element in successful organisations of the future.

6 Enhancing a single team's performance

> *Question* What did you and the team get out of the team development process?
>
> *Answer* Well, first it was valuable getting the whole team away together to establish unity of purpose. We can't do this in a normal day-to-day environment. Second, the advantage of an outside assessment, clarifying problems to be addressed. And third, a range of specific outcomes emerging from a radical rethink at a critical point in our life. That will hopefully now ensure success that would probably not have occurred without this opportunity, with dire consequences.
>
> *Member of project team*

We are constantly amazed by the sheer breadth and variety of teams that we work with or hear about. For instance there are big teams and small teams. The largest we have worked with had a core team of fifty members who in turn controlled, directly or indirectly, up to five thousand people. One of our favourites though is a team of two!

Gerard Pelisson and Paul Dubrule founded and still run the French based international hotel group Accor. They are a unique pair each bringing different backgrounds and skills to the partnership. They built their first hotel together, are now co-presidents of Accor, and are said never to take a decision without consulting each other.

There are also of course different teams at different levels within organisations. At the highest level the team is responsible for overall strategy, a very different kind of task compared to that, say, of the day-to-day operational teamwork of a stage manager's team in the theatre. The regional manager of an insurance company, with a team of branch managers, will fall somewhere in between with a mixture of local strategy formulation and responsibility for day-to-day operations.

Leaving levels aside, some of the teams that commonly need performance improvement programmes include top teams, major project teams, product or regional teams, new product development teams, joint ventures and consortiums, new venture teams and in-company project teams. These are just some of the fascinating array of teams that work within organisations.

All these teams have a job to do and are always being asked to achieve more with less. We find increasingly that teams are recognising their need for fine tuning. They want to stand back and with outside help take stock of how well they are doing and identify ways of getting even better. So also do new teams, or old teams with significant changes in leadership or membership recognise that they need to get their act together quickly and efficiently. These teams are taking a positive view of their own development. They want to accelerate the normal obstacle course of developmental steps that teams have to go through in order to reach peak performance. They want to stretch their performance to new limits. But above all, they want to get moving — and fast. Some teams however may need thorough overhauls. These are the ones that have not survived the obstacle course and are languishing, paralysed by conflict or apathy. But it is much more difficult for them to acknowledge their failings and to ask for help.

The most positive help that can be given by people such as us is in preventive medicine and improving general fitness. We help the team develop fitness regimes, some unique to its own situation and some more generally applicable to all teams. This is the team's investment in 'planning the how' of its own future success. Our role is to work jointly with the team to assess how it's working, and to discover and suggest more effective approaches. We prescribe what we know will work.

---

7 Developing Team Leaders

'It doesn't matter whether you win or you lose . . . until you lose'
George Schultz

In many organisations, it is not always possible or practical to take whole teams away for development programmes. Sometimes the response is for the consultants to spend short periods of time, such as a day, with teams on a regular basis.

Another strategy, especially where there are large numbers of teams and the organisation wants to start making an impact on all of them, is to concentrate effort on the team leaders. Organisations increasingly require a steady supply of effective team leaders and project managers to take up these important roles. Often this will involve promoting technical specialists who find these roles very demanding — sometimes too demanding. Organisations can help by providing development and training opportunities that demonstrate the complexities inherent in these roles, especially the human and organisational aspects of teamworking and project management, and how to cope successfully with them.

Groups of team leaders from within the organisation can then be assembled and a programme arranged to suit the particular needs of the organisations and of the individuals.

CREATING THE CONDITIONS FOR SUCCESS

In their formative stages Superteams are much like children. They are excitable, full of vitality, enthusiastic, inquisitive and they want to please and to excel. As with children however these positive attributes can be destroyed in a few devastating moments of misguided 'parental' behaviour.

In one company we know, the Chief Executive had been the driving force behind the introduction of a computerised ordering and control system. He believed that this would release sales managers' time which they could re-invest in developing ideas for new products and for alternative markets and uses for existing products. He called a meeting of the main people involved. It began at 9.00am. His opening remark was to express his displeasure at the poor result from a previous meeting which had been set up to address the same issue. Having made this point forcefully, he then went on to say, 'I only hope that you prove to me today that a few of you have got a bit of grey matter between your ears'. He continued to say that although the morning had been set aside for the meeting, he needed to get away sooner and would abandon the meeting at 10.00am if it was not producing the right results. The meeting inevitably was a flop with team members lapsing into a sullen and antagonistic silence and was duly abandoned at precisely 10am. An opportunity had been thrown away.

If Superteams are to be successful they must have a suitable organisation environment in which to thrive. Sometimes creating this environment confronts an organisation with challenges to its usual way of doing things. Superteams thrive in an environment which allows innovation and risk taking. Innovation is often understood intellectually but stalls because there are not the organisational skills and attitudes needed to achieve it. Risk taking is admired from afar, but given lip service when it comes to providing the support and commitment required to nurture and reward it.

In many cases, Superteams are in the front line of an organisation's attempts to grasp faster moving opportunities, where the stakes are high but the payoffs even greater. Since the level of investment in Superteams is high both materially and psychologically, they are often both highly visible and also highly vulnerable. If the stakes are greater for the organisation, so too are the stakes for a team which is expected to make a disproportionate contribution to achieving the payoffs. It is a much tougher environment in which to work. All eyes are on the team and the pressures to perform are intense.

If there is a failure in the organisation support system, the investment in Superteam strategies is often wasted. The Superteam is relegated to the league of average teams and may even fail there, unable to reconcile the high expectations set for it with the conditions allowed for it.

There is also the danger that once the Superteam strategy is employed the organisation may lose its nerve and impose restraints. The high level of uncertainty and complexity associated with Super-team activity offers a trap for the unwary. Organisations get nervous about not being able to 'see' progress in a tangible form. Especially at an early stage in the team's task, visible movement may be obscured by a high 'noise' level as the team disentangles the problem it has been given. The organisation may feel it has lost control, that the Super-team will run away unchecked and cause chaos and confusion. Most often these fears are imaginary, because they underestimate the responsibility and commitment to organisation objectives that the team has. But they are there nevertheless, and coming to terms with them is a crucial part of the role of senior management within the organisation, who are primarily responsible for creating the conditions for success. We refer to this crucial supporting role as sponsorship.

Sponsorship

We advocate that every team involved in the new teamworking strategies should have a sponsor for its activities who resides in a seat of power. The sponsor represents the organisation's needs to the team and ensures that the nature of both the opportunities and the constraints are well understood. The sponsor at times will be called upon to give clearer direction. Occasionally there may be a need to administer sanction if the team's guidelines have been overstepped, but the role is much more often a supportive one, indeed a fighting one which champions the team's cause to the rest of the organisation and secures the required resources.

Vision

A vision, in the sense in which we use it, is something to aspire to. It is not a mystical thing but a practical thing. It is a powerful and vivid picture of a desired state of affairs that is widely shared and understood and which acts like a magnet to draw people towards it.

We have already described the Superteam vision in the previous chapter; it is an ideal for teams to aspire to. In this context, however, we use the word vision to describe what an organisation or part of an organisation is trying to achieve. The vision is about purpose. It is a way of communicating the organisation's strategy and objectives so that they excite people, challenge people and attract them.

Managers can make a vision come alive by communicating it with enthusiasm and conviction. These kinds of statement provoke an immediate and positive response from Superteams. Often new teamworking strategies are part of that vision and the Superteams help to make it happen. The medium becomes part of the message.

The importance of management communicating a vision widely is that it provides unambiguous positive signals about their commitment. The vision clearly shows the ends they are striving for, and shows how Superteams are an integral part of the strategy for reaching them.

Summary

Quality of sponsorship and quality of vision are the two prime contributions that we believe managers can make to successful Superteam activity. Neither is easy and both provide new demands. In seeking to develop and improve the performance of their organisations through the use of outstanding teams, managers will themselves be challenged to develop themselves.

PART TWO
The Hallmark of Superteams

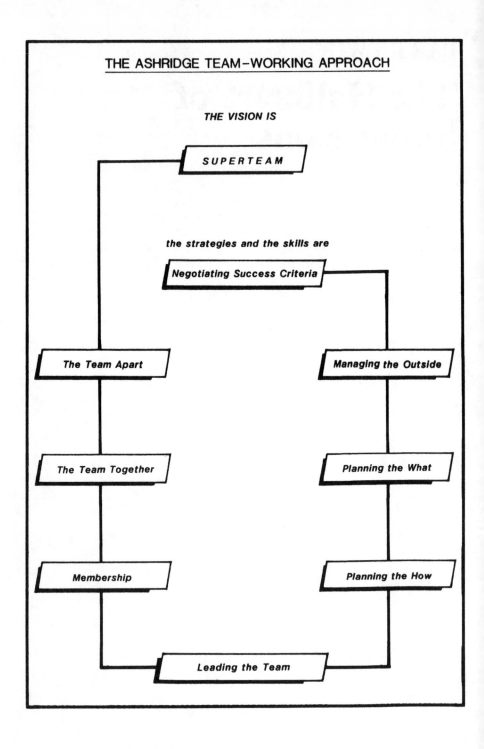

THE ASHRIDGE TEAM–WORKING APPROACH

THE VISION IS

SUPERTEAM

the strategies and the skills are

Negotiating Success Criteria

The Team Apart

Managing the Outside

The Team Together

Planning the What

Membership

Planning the How

Leading the Team

THE ASHRIDGE TEAM-WORKING APPROACH

Over a number of years, the Ashridge Team-Working Approach has proved itself as a practical way of looking at the performance of teams within organisations. It fulfils a number of useful functions.

First it provides team leaders and members with a *common team-working language* (eight straightforward concepts) that is both simple enough to remember and comprehensive enough to encompass all the complexities of team functioning. Those concepts in turn provide a *systematic approach to analysing* team performance. Analysis alone is useless without action, and so the approach is able to specify *strategies and skills that work* and contribute to outstanding performance. The approach also provides a *shared set of values and standards which characterise the Superteam's vision* and with which all teams can work.

In addition, we use the framework ourselves when consulting with teams and as the basis for developing training courses in teamworking skills. It is also useful for planning and implementing change projects in organisations. Examples of all these applications are given in Part Three.

4 Negotiating success criteria

'If you don't know where you're going, you'll probably end up somewhere else'

David Campbell

'Success is sexy'

Rosabeth Moss Kanter

'We're getting there'

British Rail advertising slogan

The most important thing to a Superteam is that they should be successful. Which of course immediately raises the question, 'what is meant by success?' Ordinary teams, in our experience, spend relatively little time thinking about the question and give simplistic answers. Superteams spend a great deal of time on it and give much more sophisticated answers.

But before we look at this in more detail, we need briefly to spell out for you some relevant assumptions that Superteams make and some particular terms that we shall be introducing.

WHO SPECIFIES SUCCESS

It's an obvious thing to say, but it's crucial to the whole thinking of Superteams. And that is that, whatever the team, it exists to satisfy the needs and expectations of one or more people *outside* the team. It is people outside the team who ultimately evaluate its performance. Teams which work purely to their own success criteria almost invariably go into decline eventually.

We use four words to describe those roles outside the team which are most significant in specifying success.

The Customer: the person or institution outside the team's organisation who takes the products, ideas or services produced by the team. Although the concept of the customer is usually associated with commercial organisations, it is equally useful to all types of organisations and teams to ask the question, 'who really wants or uses the results of what we do?'

The Client: a team may have its 'customers' within the same organisation. For instance a personnel team may see its clients as line managers. Clients therefore are customers *within* the organisation.

The Users: a computer team may be developing a new system for use in the marketing department. Their *client* is the marketing director, but the *users* are the market researchers who will operate the system on a day-to-day basis. They will have different needs and expectations.

The Sponsor(s): important people within the organisation, usually at senior levels above the team, who have 'clout'. Sponsors represent what the organisation as a whole expects from the team as well as the constraints within which the team must operate.

For instance, the technical director of one company sponsored a new product development team. The customer wanted the company to develop a new type of pump within two years. The sponsor set the scene by communicating the extreme importance of the project to the company and then outlined the amount of financial, people and production resource that the team could expect in order to build the first prototype within a year. He also made it clear that he was looking for a product that not only met the customers' requirements but was sufficiently flexible and advanced in design to meet the future needs of specified sectors in the pump market as well.

For Superteams, the simple result of these definitions is that at least initially they look outwards for their success criteria. And, as you will see, they employ some very important attitudes and skills to ensure that they get it right.

We said earlier on, that Superteams have a sophisticated view of success criteria. One of the ways in which they demonstrate this is in their awareness and understanding of the *multiple and often conflicting* sets of expectations that exist about their performance.

These differing expectations come from three main sources:

Outside — Customers, users and sponsors all have different kinds of demands that they place on teams. The customer for a new mechanical digger may be mainly interested in cost, the users in its handling and cabin comfort, and the sponsors in getting it onto the market before the competitors' new products. In addition the team may find itself having to accommodate the needs and constraints of two other important parties, sub-contractors (outside the organisation) and specialist departments (within the organisation).

Superteams are able to identify quickly the key person or people with whom negotiation of the success criteria must take place. A crucial aspect of the team leader's role is to influence and negotiate with these key people on their requirements, and to ensure that the dialogue continues on a regular basis as the situation develops or changes. If there's one thing outsiders dislike it's unpleasant surprises. Superteams ensure that they don't happen.

The team — Superteams develop their own internal success criteria. They articulate their own standards, expectations and objectives. They have their own way of summarising what needs to happen for them to be successful and how they will measure success. Superteams spend time negotiating these success criteria within the team. For instance, how is the team going to accomplish its task, who will do what and to what standards, what are the time limits and how will the team conduct itself with its customers and sponsors? This is part of what we call 'planning the how' and is covered in Chapter 7.

The individual — The team leader will also need to negotiate success criteria with each individual team member. While each member may have personal standards of performance, the leader needs to ensure that individuals understand, accept and take responsibility for their part in achieving the team's task. We find repeatedly though, that members of Superteams have their own internal standards and that often these are the toughest. Superteam members stretch themselves to do that little bit more.

For instance one UK organisation had a number of teams repairing aircraft during the Falklands War. Individuals' performance shot up by 100 per cent. There was no formal negotiation or request from the leader. Team members stretched themselves and were prepared to deliver whatever was needed.

The whole process of defining success criteria, though complex, has a very simple objective, which is to answer two questions concisely and clearly

1. What do they (outside) require from us?
2. What do we require from them?

in order that we *all* achieve what we want.

DIMENSIONS OF SUCCESS

When talking about good performance and successful achievement we find it useful to think of them along two dimensions, the hard/soft dimension and the acceptable/excellent dimension. The hard/soft dimension refers to two different kinds of *criteria* of performance, and the acceptable/excellent to two different *standards* of performance.

We find that the four combinations of criteria and standards provide a comprehensive view of what is meant by performance in any particular situation and that they are particularly useful in highlighting what is so special about outstanding performance.

The hard/soft dimension

The hard/soft dimension concerns the tangible and intangible aspects of performance. Hard criteria tend to be measurable, the most frequent being to do with time, cost, resources and technical standards. Soft criteria on the other hand are more subjective and difficult to measure. Yet they are clearly used frequently in evaluating performance. They are more about 'how' the task was accomplished, the attitudes, skills and behaviour demonstrated by the team and its members. Soft criteria often distinguish outstanding team members, for instance those who show exceptional enthusiasm or dedication. These qualities cannot really be measured — but they are real and important and there for everyone to see.

In setting success criteria ordinary teams tend to concentrate on *hard* criteria only and ask questions such as, 'How many, how much and when?' Superteams do all this too (and mostly more punctiliously) but add another dimension. They also draw out clients' and sponsors' more subtle expectations, those to do with ways of working and the relationships with the client, to attitudes adopted on such things as quality, reliability and attention to detail. These are all factors that are crucial to a client's ultimate satisfaction. Equally these soft criteria are explored, clarified and agreed with the sponsor, and service departments.

One project team spent a considerable time with its customer sifting the information the client required as and when the project unfolded. One of the important soft criteria was that the client be kept fully informed on both good news and bad news. The project manager in turn, although agreeing, was able to express some of his concerns about the arrangement. As a result he was able to secure an agreement that the client would respond promptly and frankly to the information within two days.

In another case a soft drinks firm gave a brief to its advertising agents for promoting a new fizzy drink for children. The product manager, in briefing the account executive, had said that the campaign should be 'creative, zany and summery'. When she saw their proposals she was horrified — they had produced something completely different. The account executive had assumed, wrongly, that he had understood what she required.

The acceptable/excellent dimension

The acceptable/excellent dimension on the other hand concerns standards of performance. And it is around this dimension that the whole Superteam idea was originally crystalised. In a world where the best is no longer good enough, the frontiers of performance are always being stretched. 'The best can always be bettered' could almost be the Superteam motto. We find many teams who think that their performance is good, but who in fact are underperforming. They may be averagely good when compared with those other teams they see. Their performance is acceptable but in no way outstanding.

We sometimes run a computer simulation exercise in which small teams run a company for a day in competition with each other. The success criterion they are all given is crude but very clear — *maximise profits*. When reviewing the exercise with the less successful teams, it is extraordinary how many of them discover that the criterion they were *actually* working to in practice, though never articulated, was *to minimise their losses*. This simple difference in assumption and attitude has a marked difference on the approach, style and performance of teams. More successful teams set themselves the more ambitious goals, were realistic but also prepared to take some risks. They started off by establishing minimum acceptable criteria (usually higher than the poor team's best) and then proceeded to work out how to surpass them. Superteams have this restless and inquisitive sense of being dissatisfied with what is good enough today. Superteams will 'go for bust' and 'think big'. Superteams strive to be different, and achieve just that little bit more than the competition. They are constantly looking for ways to do things better, constantly testing their assumptions about what is achievable and searching for ways to overcome any problems that lie in their path.

The leaders of Superteams have a crucial role in creating the climate where there is the commitment to being the best. It is said that Adolph Ochs, founder of the New York Times, sat silently during a meeting at which the Times Editors were congratulating themselves on their reporting of a big story. Quietly Ochs interjected by asking why another newspaper had an important angle that seemed to be missing from their paper coverage. He was met by a stunned silence. 'I want it *all*', he went on. 'Get it *right* next time'.

The chairman of an interior design company had spent three years turning the company around to achieve extremely good results once more. When asked for the magic prescription with which he mastered productivity problems he replied by sticking his hands out in front of him, palms upright and said, 'You let them know how you want it to be and you just keep pushing and pushing. I made lots of mistakes and admitted them. But I still kept pushing'.

The distinctions between hard and soft criteria and acceptance and excellent standards are crucial ones. Superteams, while committed to technical excellence are also committed to getting all the other soft intangibles outstandingly good — the combination is a rare and much sought after attribute — all round quality.

CONTRACTING

The process of arriving at success criteria is an intricate and skilled one because there is a lot happening under the surface. On the surface the team is simply asking the client or sponsor what is wanted. Simple enough you might say. But we have seen repeatedly how clients are poor at articulating what they want — until they see something they don't want — remember our horrified fizzy drink product manager! Perhaps she hadn't been very clear. But then neither had the account executive been skilful in drawing out and clarifying what she wanted. Those in Superteams who are skilful at handling clients are like detectives at work. They are probing for clues as to what the clients want, and putting together different bits of evidence to build up a clear comprehensive and deep understanding of their needs and requirements. They understand that clients have often not given a lot of thought to what they want or simply don't know. They help their clients to formulate a picture. Often they will make their own suggestions to test out a clients reaction; another excellent way of helping clients clarify what they do or don't want.

At another level, the relationship is being developed and cemented at this stage. In exploring the success criteria together, it is evident that both parties have a stake in the project. The interdependence between the client and the team becomes clearer and the bond should become stronger. Superteams are striving to get close to their customers and sponsors; indeed we would go so far as saying that they see the customer as an integral and useful member of their team making a key contribution to its success.

At yet another level each side is testing the other one out, assessing capabilities and looking for weaknesses. The most exacting instances of these that we have come across tend to occur in high technology military projects, where the client subjects would be contractors to a widespread and searching scrutiny to assess their overall ability to deliver. The managing director of GEC Avionics, after being awarded a major contract by the US Army and Navy, described how he and his team were questioned on every aspect of their company "It was like being put through a wringer" he said.

Another kind of testing goes on where there is disagreement over what is needed or how it should be done. Under these circumstances those working with the client and sponsors needs to be good at *negotiating* in order to resolve the issues to the satisfaction of *both* parties. A common mistake is that teams, sponsors and clients avoid or gloss over their differences hoping that 'it'll be alright on the night', often with serious consequences. Superteams don't avoid issues, they face them head on.

We refer to this process of developing the relationship and arriving at success criteria as 'contracting'. It is a subtle process through which trust and confidence is developed between the parties, and through which real understanding is reached by both sides about what is expected of the other. It is therefore a two way process.

The word 'contracting' as we use it has no legalistic overtones although a legal contract may or may not result from it. We are concerned with 'contracting' as a process. It's about exploring and getting agreement on what each party expects of the other; it's about understanding realistically the constraints of the other party; it's about communicating success criteria to each other and it's about defining some simple rules on how the relationship is to work: but above all, it's the best means of developing clarity in the relationship, both at a technical and personal level, in order to avoid any nasty surprises in the future. A multinational consortium was awarded a contract in the Middle East. The success criteria were simple — to design and build a new zoo. When the first people arrived on site they got two shocks. First, they found an old zoo, and second they found animals in it! The clients had assumed they knew and that the plan catered for moving the animals. The consortium had never visited the site and didn't think to ask.

In the best relationships a mutual respect and robustness is developed between the parties that stands them in good stead. Each can be frank and tough with the other. Each can make demands of the other and each sees the other as an ally. In the worst relationships, the team sees the client or sponsor as an enemy or a nuisance and the client or sponsor sees the team as incompetent. In our experience this happens when teams don't think or care enough about what their clients want. There are bad clients — and bad sponsors — but the team is ultimately responsible for that relationship. If they really can't work for a client or sponsor they should discover that at the contracting stage and deal with the problem or pull out.

Superteam leaders and members don't cut corners in getting their contracting right. They put a great deal of effort in, in the expectation of getting a great deal out. One specialised shipbuilding project involved a joint venture with a large chemical company and close involvement with a firm of consulting engineers as subcontractors. The clients project team was involved in protracted and sometimes painful discussions and negotiations for six months before the final contract was signed. In this case the contract not only covered the usual technical, financial and legal elements but also spelt out agreed organisation structures, reporting procedures and control systems amongst others. Despite the difficulties, the parties come out closely knit and very committed to their common objective.

THE LURE OF SUCCESS

The process of contracting lays the foundation for any team's success. Contracting with customer or clients provides the first pillar, and contracting with the organisation of which the team is part provides the second pillar for future achievement. Get these wrong or weak and the edifice collapses as the fabric of the building begins to be assembled. However, get them right and you have a strong partnership between team, client and organisation. That is why Superteams which exist to succeed understand contracting so well and put so much energy into this kind of groundwork. The word failure is not in their vocabulary — just what do we have to do to achieve the right results? Start with contracting is the answer.

For Superteams, the excitement of planning how to succeed and the vision of future success provide an irresistible form of motivation. But Superteams are adept at exploiting it even further. Because they realise the enormous power of successful achievement to motivate people, they build in frequent opportunities for team members to see and experience successes as they go along. We call these milestones, clear markers along the route signalling that parts of the journey have been successfully accomplished.

Superteams therefore set themselves up for success by doing good groundwork in contracting, aim for success in the form of clearly articulated and understood success criteria and celebrate and make visible successes and achievements as they go along. This way members can continually see where they are going and look back with satisfaction at where they come from. There is a feeling of progress. We hope to show you in the following chapters how this philosophy gets translated right down to the way that the team as a whole works and the way individual team members manage and are managed.

Negotiating success criteria
Suggestions for Superteams

TWO SETS OF EARS, EYES AND BRAINS ARE BETTER THAN ONE

When talking to clients and sponsors in particular, send at least *two* people from the team. The single person has an enormous burden to try to listen, interpret, clarify, record, negotiate and suggest quite apart from subsequently reporting all of that back to the team completely, accurately and objectively.

Two people can help each other in various ways.

- One acts as recorder and clarifier while the other talks.
- Straight after the meeting they compare notes and recollections.
- In reporting back they help each other to describe factually and precisely what they heard.

DRAWING THE CLIENT OR SPONSOR OUT — SOME USEFUL QUESTIONS

Basics	What are the basic things we must do?
Fantasy	If we were to be satisfying your most outrageous hopes totally, what sort of things would we be doing?
Constraints	Is there anything that you don't want us to do or that we must not do?
Other people	Is there anyone else besides you who may have views about what's needed?
Quality	What does quality mean for you?
Kite flying	Is there anything else we haven't asked you about that we should know?

REALISM AND OPPORTUNISM

1 *Realism* If the client's or sponsor's expectations are unrealistic (that is, they want too much too soon) then either negotiate the demands down or negotiate for more resource or time. If you complain, they won't be convinced. If you're assertive and back up your case with well reasoned arguments, they'll thank you for saving them future problems.

2 *Opportunism* If you think the client's or sponsor's expectations are too low, then tell them. Don't opt for the easy life. Show them how they can benefit from better quality or by producing the same quality with fewer people, money or time. They will appreciate your enabling them to enhance their perceived achievements.

HARD SPECS AND SOFT SPECS

A technical specification or brief and sometimes a plan is commonly used as a summary of a team's success criteria. But it's only half the story.

Try writing a Soft Criteria Spec. and making it available to all members of the team. Better still, have meetings involving everyone in the team in which the clients' and sponsors' Soft Criteria are explained and discussed until everyone has a clear and common understanding of them.

5 Managing the outside

Project team member: 'The customer said she wants a hi-tech innovative solution to the problem. Ours is boring and conventional.'

Project Manager: 'Yes, yes I know it is — but it's up to the marketing people to make it *sound* different'

Clients on teamworking programme

Getting close to the customer is a real winner

Tom Peters, quoting one of his clients

No team can be successful using its own resources alone. Teams which become purely inward looking eventually fail because they lose contact with what's going on around them. In other words, teams need to look outwards as well as inwards if they are to excel at what they are doing. Superteams do not merely look outwards — they lay considerable importance on the positive management of key relationships outside the team.

THE INVISIBLE TEAM

In the previous chapter, 'Negotiating Success Criteria', we described how key roles outside the team, such as customers, clients, users and sponsors, had expectations of the team and made demands of it. There is, however, another side to these roles. For not only do they demand, they also provide. Each of these external roles, and others besides, if managed well, contributes significantly to the team's success. We refer to them as the invisible team.

The client or customer — an invaluable source of guidance, information and ideas but one which is sadly neglected by many teams. Many teams are beginning to see and treat their clients and customers as members of the team.

The sponsor — has a crucial positive role as godfather, mentor, fixer, smoother, promoter and resource provider for the team. A good sponsor ensures that the wider organisation gives full support to the team and is an invaluable asset.

Service departments — other specialist functions within the organisation who have information, expertise or people that the team may need to call on in order to get its job done well.

Subcontractors — specialists outside the organisation who may be called on to perform part of the team's task.

Gatekeepers — people inside and outside the organisations who have access to important or useful people or knowledge. Gatekeepers open doors.

One new product development team which consisted of only six full time people, had to make extensive use of specialists within the organisation from sales and marketing, computer and accounts to production engineering and personnel. Externally they had to appoint specialist consulting engineers to design electronic control systems and subcontractors to make them. They also had considerable contact with two university research departments on new advanced light-weight materials and new bearing and lubrication technologies. All in all, the core team was managing a significant invisible team of outside specialists and probably many others besides, and it was the team's responsibility to ensure that those outsiders were as dedicated to the success of the project as they were. That is the key issue in managing the outside: how to mobilise and motivate people outside the team towards achieving the team's objectives.

IMAGE

Remember that the attitude and behaviour of people outside towards the team are partly governed by their perceptions of the team. One team we worked with had been set up to design and build the onshore and offshore installations for an under-sea gas field. Negotiations with the customer for the gas were complex and more protracted than expected but nevertheless the design was going ahead. Key members of the team were frustrated by the delay but were shocked to learn that their project was being viewed within the organisation as a potential failure and questions were being asked about its viability. The project had not at that stage needed a lot of external resources and had become inward looking. The result was that the only messages that they had communicated externally were of gloom and despondency. This was not in fact how they felt but unwittingly they had succeeded in creating the situation where the sponsors support would be withdrawn and the company would reassess the future of the project.

Limited information

People outside form their view of a team by drawing inferences and conclusions from the information they have. The most common situation is that they have little or no information about the team, especially if it's a new one. In these circumstances outsiders will make assumptions or rumours. It is vital therefore that the team takes active steps to ensure that important outsiders have an accurate image of what the team does, what it stands for and how it may affect their roles. The team's image determines its credibility with outsiders and its credibility in turn plays a large part in determining whether other people's attitudes are going to be positive, indifferent or at worst hostile.

Both leaders and members therefore need to pay attention to the team's external image. Outstanding team leaders and members realise that they are all the team's ambassadors, for it is mostly through personal contact that images are formed and confidence and trust developed. However, it is also through the written word and other communications that impressions are created. If the team leader's memos are poorly thought out and poorly typed, others will draw their own conclusions. If letters or requests for information are not promptly replied to, the impression becomes 'fact'.

For the top team in an organisation there are often two important external relationships where the team's image is very important — the stock market and the media. Many business organisations put significant resource and effort into briefing investment analysts on a regular basis. One of our clients is a small company in a sector that recently suffered a sharp decline in share prices. The drop was the result of problems in large companies in the sectors, but our clients found their price being pulled down too. They immediately mounted two open days at their main factory during which the whole Board was involved in briefing 150 investment analysts about the company's performance and prospects.

Many top teams view the media with mild paranoia. Often this attitude results from bad experiences suffered by people ill-prepared to meet the medias demands. But used skilfully, the press and television can contribute enormously to the image of an organisation. A spectacular example is the way that Bob Geldof used the international media to promote the giant rock concert, Live Aid. Conversely, the European pharmaceutical industry has been criticised for always being suspicious and on the defensive with the media rather than taking a more positive approach and, for example, providing the media with examples of its successes.

BUILDING CONNECTIONS

The old cliché 'it's not what you know but who you know' is both right and wrong when applied to effective teamworking. What people know is a vital element in the contribution that they make to the team. But Superteams are keenly aware of what they *don't* know or cannot do and its at this time that who they know becomes crucial.

Rosabeth Moss Kanter, Professor of Organisation and Management at Yale University, in her recent study of successful corporate entrepreneurs *The Change Masters*, found that these managers were excellent at systematically building up their connections inside and outside the organisation. The result was that they always had access to a network of people who could help. This was one of the secrets behind their ability to get things done where others failed.

We have noticed a very similar process with the most highly regarded project managers, team leaders and team members. There seem to be two main strategies behind their cultivation of connections.

(i) *Search for specific expertise* — probably the most common, this strategy is designed to fill the gaps in the team's knowledge and experience. In addition to the normal connections, consultants, agencies and specialised computer databases are increasingly being used to provide help. A small publishing company, for instance, has recently won the contract to market a database internationally which records all the scientific research taking place in the UK Universities and Government research establishments.

(ii) *Creative search* — using outsiders (sometimes deliberately unconnected with the team's work) to examine and challenge the team's work. This is an excellent way of ensuring that the team's thinking does not get stuck in a rut. Tom Peters (co-author of *In Search of Excellence*), reviewing the performance of America corporate strategy departments, concludes that the most significant new ideas come not from within, but from teams that went out and asked the users what they wanted.

Through an active process of building connections with outsiders, effective teams utilise a powerful and varied network of experience and expertise to help them to be successful.

PREPARING THE GROUND

Before the invisible team can be expected to contribute to the objectives of the team, there is considerable groundwork to be done. After all, why should they be committed to someone elses objectives? In our experience this commitment has to be earned. The most productive relationships are those which are clear, demanding and supportive on both sides.

Being clear — whether the team is dealing with subcontractors outside the organisation or other departments within the organisation it is crucial that both sides are clear about what each expects of the other. Success criteria, both hard and soft, are discussed extensively and agreed. So too are the ground rules for identifying and resolving misunderstandings and differences.

Being demanding — Superteams set high standards for themselves and expect the same of others. But equally they encourage others to be demanding of *them* recognising that they too have a role to play in the performance of others. For instance, one client agreed with its subcontractors to answer all queries on specifications within twenty-four hours.

Being supportive — Superteams recognise that they have a vested interest in providing all the help that they can to others. They acknowledge that the relationship is reciprocal. For instance one international oil company seconded one of its own specialists to its subcontractor to work alongside them on a critical development.

Resolving differences

Of course not everything goes smoothly even when the groundwork has been done. And it is then that the difference between those who are good at managing the outside, and those who are not becomes apparent. Those who are poor may feel impotent; they may passively accept the situation and perhaps compromise standards. Alternatively they may resort to hostility and look for someone to blame. Those who are good however respond positively to solve the problems. They capitalise on their connections, and the credits that they have built up. They use their ability to influence and to persuade others. They use their ability to negotiate with others. They use their ability to see creative ways round problems and search for alternative solutions. They *share* the problem by saying how are 'we' going to solve it? Ultimately, in order to achieve a solution they are prepared to cash in some of their credit by being insistent and demanding, (and often unpopular) but secure in the knowledge that their relationships are robust enough to stand up to this treatment.

MOBILISING RESOURCES

The reason why Superteams put so much effort into building connections and preparing the ground is to ensure that they can get what they want when they want it. Because they drive themselves hard and work to tight time deadlines, they need to have all the pieces of the jigsaw ready well in advance. It's too late to wait until they are needed.

The most common tangible resources that the team is trying to secure are people, money, materials, time and information. In order to be sure of obtaining these, Superteams prepare the ground assiduously in order to mobilise intangible resources — by that we mean the confidence, trust, ideas and active support of those outside the team.

Getting the right people

Team leaders and sponsors who have an extensive network of connections inside and outside the organisation are already one step ahead in the race for resources. They are particularly well placed because they know the people who would be able to make the best contribution to their team.

But in selecting people, the leaders and sponsors of Superteams are not only on the lookout for specialist knowledge. They are equally concerned to assess the individuals' teamworking ability, the unique contribution that they could make to *how* the team works, as opposed to *what* it does. Equally if they are recruiting from outside they ensure that these two broad criteria are reflected in advertisements or briefs to recruitment agencies. One of us was working with the Chief Officer of a government agency to help select a new administrative director. While describing the administrative and financial skills required for the post, he suddenly stopped and said, 'What I *really* need too, is a person who brings new ideas. We're short of those in the team'. In the event there were two applicants with the necessary technical experience. As a result of interviews and a short teamworking questionnaire, we were able to say confidently that one of them was a much better ideas person than the other. She got the job.

Accumulating credit and building trust

Teams need to built up credit with outsiders in preparation for the time they need help from them. Leaders and members build credit by being visible to others. They show that they understand the outsiders' situation and pressures, letting them know of demands on them well in advance and explaining why they want things. These are all ways of storing credit so that when the team wants things done they happen quickly, efficiently and to the satisfaction of both parties. Once outsiders have developed confidence in the ability and credibility of the team, then negotiating for other resources such as money, materials and time becomes easier. Likewise information flows more openly and smoothly when the relationship is good.

The process of building credit is particularly crucial for any new team within an organisation, and especially a new one involved with any innovation within the organisation. For the most important resource in this situation is the support for *the idea* of the team amongst the senior decision makers in the organisation. At this early stage leader and members are acting as champions of their idea and are engaged in a process of informing others, understanding and overcoming their objections, understanding the factions and motives of the different parties involved, lobbying and persuading these key figures how the idea can benefit the organisation.

In one university department, a small team of academics wanted to launch an innovative new programme. They spent nearly eight months gaining the commitment of key decision makers within the university. Doubters and dissenters made the going hard right up to the final decision. But having put effort and thought into this preparation and the subsequent agreement, implementation was achieved smoothly with the full co-operation of all concerned.

The effect on the team

There is one other important and rather subtle spin-off for the leaders and members who are good at managing the outside. Rosabeth Moss Kanter found that managers who were good at securing resources were seen as credible and influential by their colleagues and staff. Furthermore these colleagues not only developed greater respect for the influential managers, but felt that their own status and confidence was enhanced by being in the same team. In other words, effective management of the outside has a positive motivational effect not only on outsiders, but also within the team itself. We have found this to be particularly the case when a team sees its work well publicised. The publicity breeds pride, and the pride reinforces commitment.

INSIDERS AND OUTSIDERS

There is always a danger of a 'them and us' attitude developing which is a great threat to effective teamworking.

Competitiveness

One of the realities in organisations is that there are limited resources and that different teams or departments are competing for a share of the available resources. While a certain amount of competition is healthy, too much has consequences which are not only bad for the teams, but more importantly bad for the organisation as a whole;

- each team tends to become more inward looking
- each team starts seeing the others in a negative light
- hostility between teams increases while contact and communication decrease
- perceptions become distorted; each group only sees the good bits about itself and the bad bits about others.

The consequences for effective mobilisation of resources outside a team are obvious. If the overall climate in an organisation has become one of distrust and suspicion between different departments it is very difficult for even the best leader and most positive members to overcome. In many such situations, external teamworking consultants are used. They bring people from different departments together to examine the conflicts and to work out ways of creating a more positive and co-operative climate.

Arrogance

A particular danger facing Superteams is that they often become very cohesive and confident and in so doing may unwittingly put up barriers to those outside. Confidence may turn to arrogance; they begin to appear like some exclusive club which denies membership to others, and become dismissive of others' abilities and achievements. They may actually cause envy and hostility from others.

Conflicting priorities

On a day-to-day basis there are and there will always be conflicts of priorities between a team and outsiders. In one photographic organisation, there were a number of different lines each cutting and packaging different types of film and photographic paper. Three departments each had a number of lines.

The maintenance department served all three. The inevitable horror happened, as one machine broke down in each department simultaneously. Each of the departmental team leaders insisted that their breakdown was the most urgent. A lot of heat was generated and time lost as each leader pushed for priority. Should the high volume, high value, low margin line be repaired first? Or should the small volume, high margin line take priority? Or should the line doing a special order for an important new customer, already a day overdue be first. The situation was not resolved until one of the team leaders suggested a quick meeting with their immediate boss, the production manager, the sales manager and the maintenance manager. They straight away contacted the warehouse manager to ascertain stocks, and very quickly decided that the company's best interests were served by meeting the special order for the new customer first and then doing the line with lowest stock. This is a fine example of bringing together the invisible team, all of them with a common problem, to make joint decisions, to decide priorities, and to resolve problems.

Managing the Outside

Suggestions for Superteams

1 THE RESOURCE AUDIT

- List all the areas of expertise that your team might possibly require to be successful.
- Identify the gaps in the team's knowledge, experience and resources.
- Brainstorm names of people whom team members know or know of that may be able to help in each area.
- Compile a directory and circulate it round the whole team.

WINNERS AND LOSERS

- Identify and list those people who are going to be most affected (positively or negatively) by what your team is doing.
- Allocate responsibility for developing each relationship particularly with those people who may feel they are going to be adversely affected by what your team is doing.

2 MARKETING THE TEAM

Inside the organisation
- Arrange formal presentations for the invisible team with good quality visual aids.
- Hold informal question and answer sessions.
- Issue written material explaining the why, what, when, who and how of the team.
- Ask important outsiders what they see as the strengths and weaknesses of the team.

- Tell them what you are doing about the weaknesses.
- Publicise the team's successes.
- Maintain constant personal contact.

Outside the Organisation. Many of the above; but in addition
- Create exhibition stands and materials.
- Make a video film explaining the team's work.
- Inform national and trade press.
- Organise open house days for customers, suppliers, subcontractors, gatekeepers and other opinion leaders.

---

3 US AND THEM — DANGER SIGNALS

- Avoid stereotyping

  'They're a lazy bunch in that department. No one could care less'.

- Avoid generalisations

  'Production always deliver late. You can never rely on them'.

- Avoid offloading blame

  'It's not our fault. We've done our bit. It's their problem now, not ours'.

6 Planning the what

'IBM, in developing the PC, beat the PC industry's development norm of twenty-four months by almost ten months and its own previous timescales on bigger machines by almost three years . . . For some electronic companies slipping twelve months in development can reduce by fifty per cent the revenue generated by a product over its entire life'

Christopher Lorenz
Financial Times

CHALLENGING MEDIOCRITY

Following the Falklands war in 1982, fierce controversy broke out over the award of the contract to refit the liner Cunard Countess (used as a troopship during the campaign) to a Maltese yard. Shipyards in Britain had been invited to tender for the work, which involved converting the ship back to its peace time cruise role. All said it was impossible to meet the tough forty-four day deadline set by Cunard. The Maltese completed the refit within the deadline and in beating all the odds, boosted their yard's morale at a difficult period for all shipyards.

So, the supposedly impossible clearly is achievable. But how? Perhaps the best place to start is by looking at what stops team leaders and members from *believing* that they can achieve the impossible. One of the blockages we believe lies in some of the techniques and attitudes that ordinary teams use in planning, the consequences of which lead them to believe that they cannot achieve a deadline. Superteams on the other hand, using the same techniques, but in a very different way and with different attitudes, have no such pessimism and defeatism. Faced with an impossible goal, they will apply enormous energy to searching for ways of getting there. Their optimism and commitment boosts their confidence and provides the creative impetus to succeed.

Conventional planning is typically viewed as a process of making sure that what is intended actually happens. It stresses outcomes and in doing so concerns itself with defining tasks and activities, allocating resources and setting budgets and deadlines. Planners employ analytical techniques such as critical path analysis to predict and control what happens by visualising the order of activities, how long each should take, the order in which they should occur and how they relate to each other. This main focus we call *planning the what*. Although vitally necessary, as a means to an end, Superteams realise that Planning the What alone is insufficient to guarantee achievement. It has to be complemented by a widely neglected and undervalued part of the planning process which we refer to as *planning the how*. Planning the How is concerned with motivating, energising, and securing the commitment of the team to the 'what'. Planning the How is about programming the team for success. Like a computer with poor software programmes, a team which does not plan the how will fail to meet the high expectations set for it even though the goal and the plan for getting there may be quite clear. We talk about Planning the How in the next chapter.

In this and the next chapter therefore, we shall be describing the different approaches and attributes Superteams bring to planning. Whereas ordinary teams accept and value a plan as an end in itself, an instruction about what will happen, Superteams value the *process* of planning where the plan itself is merely a tool, a means to an end. In planning the how, they are often challenging their own plan and reformulating it if they can see a better way. Through this process, what once seemed impossible becomes feasible. And it is these differences of approach and attitude to planning that we believe give Superteams a great deal of their edge, their ability to achieve in practice what in the minds of others remains impossible. The respective attitudes of a team to planning the what and the how have a crucial bearing on whether it is to be condemned to mediocrity or elevated to the Superteam league.

MAKING ENEMIES OUT OF FRIENDS

Two professional planners in a new product development team worked hard to perfect their plan for the team's programme over the next two-and-a-half years. They used sophisticated computer techniques to help them. Excited by their achievement, which was of the highest professional standard, they enthusiastically unveiled the plan to the team. No one could deny the effort that had gone into preparing the precision and detail shown in the plan, which emerged as a computer printout stretching round three walls of the room where it was presented. To the bewilderment of the planners however, the immediate response of the rest of the team was hostile, cynical and dismissive. Many questioned its value since they couldn't understand it. Others felt it had few roots in the real world in which they operated. Some took the attitude that the plan was a painful ritual which had to be gone through, but which would bear little resemblance to what actually happened. The planners and the rest of the team were left resentful, embittered and alienated. In this instance, perhaps unusually, the plan was not even accepted in a resigned and cynical fashion. It was rejected.

Luckily for this newly formed team they were able to seize the opportunity to look at what had gone wrong and to develop a mutually acceptable alternative. What were their conclusions?

A plan for failure

The intention behind the plan had been to provide a way for the team to monitor its performance against expectations. The planners had genuinely wanted to make a positive contribution to giving the team direction and keeping it on track. Instead, it was widely perceived as being a mechanism for catching people out and focusing blame when things went wrong. It pushed team members to take action reluctantly rather than pulling out their genuine commitment.

Closely linked to this was the feeling that the planners, who themselves would have little part in its implementation, would stand back and demand credit in the event of success but would blame the team in the event of failure. They found it difficult to accept the team's view that they and the plan were part of the problem and should carry some of the responsibility for failure as well as success.

Team members also pointed out how in the past, sophisticated plans developed solely by planners had become ends in themselves rather than the means to achieving goals. Pressure has been exerted to remain faithful to the planners plan as being the 'best' route, even in the face of growing evidence of more efficient alternatives that emerged as the task went along. The result was that, rather than supporting success, the plan was viewed as a set of inflexible demands on how the team should use its time and resources and imposed severe constraints on the leader's and members' authority to influence changes in the best interests of the project.

The painful experience of this team taught us and them the blindingly obvious; that the *process* used to develop plans is a fundamental factor in determining whether the team believes in them. And it demonstrated that if the team doesn't believe in them, they won't happen. It also demonstrated, after the team had all worked on examining the plan together, that collectively they were able to come up with some radical approaches which resulted in a far more efficient programme and an earlier delivery to the customer.

The secret of success

Our conclusion from this episode and many others, is that when teams say that something is impossible that they are creating a self-fulfilling prophecy. What they frequently mean is first, that they haven't searched hard enough for alternative approaches that will make it possible and second, that they do not know how to mobilise the commitment of their team to believing that it is possible. It is these two factors that Superteams excel at when they are planning the what and planning the how.

In Superteams, Planning the What is a joint venture between planners and doers. The whole team engages in planning right from the beginning. Misunderstandings are put right, doubts are checked out, the language of planning is brought down to earth with the result that assimilation of the plan is vastly speeded up. The whole team feels ownership of the plan — it becomes 'our' plan not 'their' plan. Teams which are included in the planning process become the most dedicated supporters and ardent self-critics. They become committed to continuous improvement and to ultimate success.

PLANNING THE KNOWN

Planning forecasts the future. It provides a set of predictions about what ought to happen at some distant point in time. It cannot deal in certainty, only in probabilities, and its success depends heavily on choosing the right assumptions to work with.

Sometimes the way ahead is relatively clear to all concerned. There is extensive past experience of what is to be done, and no significant change is expected in the conditions under which it is to be done.

Even in the hostile conditions of the North Sea, the third and fourth platforms developed by BP were more predictable and routine than the first two. The lessons had been learned. In planning next year's production of tinned baked beans the market is realistically expected to stay fairly predictable. Data on trends in consumption are available, the technology is familiar. Here planning becomes an extension of the present. The team can work with its existing knowledge, knowing how long jobs take, what resources will be needed and what kinds of problems are likely to occur.

Linear logic

Even when planning the known however, there are significant differences in the way that a Superteam works. Ordinary teams use linear thinking. They have in their heads a model which shows a number of logical steps, each preceded and followed by others in a linear sequence. The first link in the chain has to be completed before the next can begin. The customer specification is agreed with marketing before design works on it. Design complete before handing over to production engineering who in turn finalise their work before handing over to production.

Superteams, however, see this as very cumbersome and inefficient and instead plan for parallel implementation. That is to say they take risks in starting up one activity before earlier ones are completed. They start as much as they can as early as they can and have all specialisms involved. In this way they learn fast and they learn together. They also use parallel implementation as an early warning system to identify problems which arise in the early stages and which would only show up later in the linear model. In this way they stay flexible. Parallel implementation combined with a lot of communication between specialisms keeps the whole team in touch in ways which reinforce commitment to the goal and stimulate the continuing search for better ways of getting there.

One international manufacturer of packaged goods responded to rapidly increasing competition by changing its whole attitude to new product development. Its teams used to market test the completely developed product on two million customers over two years before deciding whether to go ahead and invest in new plant and equipment. Market testing is now conducted very quickly, and more often, on as few as two thousand consumers as the product definition evolves. Work is started on new production plant and equipment ordering at the same time as market testing is being carried out. This parallel implementation is a more high risk approach, but one which can halve the development-to-production cycle from eight to four years. The research and development manager puts the issue succinctly — 'The World no longer sits around waiting for you to upscale production'.

The Big Picture

The highest level of planning in superteams, creates what we call the Big Picture, a snap-shot of the team's total activity. It is essentially a simple outline that can be understood very quickly. It is often complemented by commentary which gives important background information. It will also pin-point important targets and be candid in pointing out likely problem areas and who is going to be involved in dealing with them. It is not the sole property of a privileged few at the top, but is a public declaration of intent, widely available to all team members. Its purpose is to ensure that everyone has a common picture and understanding of the essentials. It is constantly monitored and updated. It forms the team's overall strategy for reaching its objective.

The Big Picture fulfils a number of important functions for Superteams. First it paints a vivid image of what's important in a simple way. It sets out the broad priorities. Secondly it demonstrates a commitment to openness. The emphasis is on full communication, on ensuring understanding of the plan, both inside and outside the team. It defines the team's core activities, and stimulates debate and feedback on how to proceed. It is therefore a crucial mechanism for gaining and checking commitment.

The third function of the Big Picture is to put the plan in context. Team members need to know why things are being done in certain ways. In small teams communicating context is relatively easy, but in larger and especially in highly dispersed teams, a conscious effort has to be made. One team for example was responsible for developing a new onshore oil-field in an area of outstanding natural beauty. Faced with powerful opposition, it became crucial to success that all team members fully understood the importance and implications of satisfying the local community and pressure groups on ecological and environmental safeguards.

Lower levels of planning

Superteams decentralise the bulk of planning. Rather than working from one comprehensive plan combining everything, they acknowledge the value of multiple plans, each focusing on a different level of the teams activities. Each level becomes more detailed as the process gets closer to those members who are responsible for implementation. They will be involved in developing their plans jointly with planners, thus ensuring that best use is made of the relevant expertise held by team members.

Secondary planning specialists who are often located within sub-teams, put detail on the big picture. Their aim is operational effectiveness. The number of levels below the big picture is flexible and obviously related to the complexity of the teams total task.

Within Superteams, the development and monitoring of these more detailed plans is the responsibility of the sub-teams themselves. It is up to them to find the best way of reaching their immediate objectives, within the overall parameters set by the next level of planning above them. In this way Superteams can retain flexibility while dealing with very real complexity. This system of planning the what however, cannot work without sophisticated ground rules for communication within the team. Which is why only Superteams, with their mechanisms for rapid communication, can make it work.

PLANNING THE UNKNOWN

Superteams, by their very nature, are often confronted with situations and demands that have not been met before. It is as if they are walking in thick fog to new destinations, where past experience may not help too much in making accurate predictions about the future. It is under these conditions that Superteams are at their unconventional best in flouting conventional planning wisdom.

Moving quickly

When faced with the unknown or uncertain Superteams don't plan much at all. They know that to try to plan too deep too early in the face of high uncertainty will surely paralyse them. They recognise the perils of trying to predict the unpredictable. They also know that the most effective way of reducing uncertainty is to *do* things. They try things out to see what happens and if it doesn't work the first time they make a different approach. The Superteam uses its Big Picture plan as the stimulus for developing hunches about the areas of greatest uncertainty. Like many major breakthroughs in science, big successes often come from 'following your nose' rather than from a rigid adherence to a plan. By doing things by quick sorties into the fog Superteams learn quickly about the nature of the terrain that they have to cross.

Moreover, Superteams are busy using parallel implementation at this early stage. Small task forces are out all at the same time, tentatively probing different regions in the zone of uncertainty. They don't stay out long, and return frequently to pool their growing experience, to build up a common data base and to look for important patterns, connections and ideas which give them clues about where and how to proceed.

A client of ours was faced with the alarming prospect of having to deliver a sophisticated and innovative new product concept to their customer within six months. Central planning department, charged with mapping a way through the unknown did so with the most modern aids at its disposal. The team which had been specially put together to produce the prototype knew differently. Reaching the target on time would have been difficult enough even with previous experience. Confronted with the need to meet entirely new performance criteria for the product in a form which had never been made before, the team was faced with the 'impossible'.

They realised that they needed to have direct and frequent dialogue with the customer to short-circuit delays in getting feedback. The central plan denied them this on the grounds that that was the role of the marketing department. They also decided that they needed to bring specialists from the customer organisation to work with their craftsmen on developing prototypes directly without formal design drawings. Again the plan established a formal sequence of communication from customer to marketing to design and then to craftsmen which would have added days of delay in transforming ideas into hardware. When it finally became clear to the sponsor that the team needed to 'break the rules', the formal plan was abandoned.

Suddenly things began to happen. A creative dam burst. There was a huge increase in movement and contacts between departments and between team and client. Small sub-groups of different specialists had hurried meetings, made quick decisions and tried them out at once. The team rapidly discovered what it knew and what it didn't know and concentrated its resources accordingly. All of a sudden visible progress was being made as one milestone after another was passed. This fuelled the team's excitement and they delivered on time after a hectic dash to the finishing line.

Plan–Do cycles

Superteams not only make sorties into the unknown very early on as a way of developing understanding but they continue to do so. As the early low-level sorties help them to build up a more reliable picture of the unknown territory, so their later sorties are based on greater knowledge and the ability to predict and plan the detail of what they are to do with greater confidence.

We use the term plan–do cycles to describe the Superteams frequent and often relatively short periods of immersion in doing, each followed by a period of reflection, sharing of knowledge gained and consolidation before the team moves forward again. Each cycle of planning and doing builds on earlier ones. Each successive planning phase feeds on the latest intelligence information gained by all the team which in turn enables the team to see further ahead.

The payoff from early plan–do cycles is usually enormous. Combining plan–do with parallel implementation within the parameters of a simple Big Picture, proves a powerful strategy for helping a team manager uncertainty. However their use is not confined to the uncertain. In more familiar territory, these tools enable Superteams to cut swathes through the inefficiencies of the linear approach, which is still so widely practised in organisations.

To summarise then, uncertainty for Superteams is reduced by doing, not by planning. Surprises are expected, not unexpected. The Big Picture points the team in the right general direction and serves to brief members on core activities and deadlines. It also indicates areas of uncertainty. Frequent plan–do cycles operating in parallel on a broad front reduce uncertainty. They also enable the team to plan; initially fairly short term, but later more long term, more realistically and with increasing precision, thereby increasing the certainty of reaching the team's goal.

MILESTONES NOT MILLSTONES

Conventional plans set targets or milestones at large intervals at which points the performance of individuals and teams is judged. These judgements are reasonable indicators of performance when a team is functioning in relatively certain conditions. They are less reliable or fair when the team is dealing with considerable uncertainty or unpredictability. At worst the team feels set up for failure. It is given unrealistic targets to meet, based on the arbitrary assumptions and predictions of some planner. If the team then does not meet the target, it is seen as their fault and they experience failure and perhaps punishment. Furthermore, as the team gets more feedback about the increasing likelihood of failure, it begins to invest more of its energies into covering its tracks, blaming others and managing its ever more delicate relationship with the sponsor. The team works with a millstone round its neck.

Superteams don't fall into this trap. They capitalise on the Big Picture map and plan–do cycles to set *themselves* ambitious but realistic milestones. But the key difference is that their milestones will always be in sight. A milestone that can be seen is a much greater motivator than one over the horizon that cannot be seen. Superteams set limited but realistic milestones for each core activity within the Big Picture. The end of each core activity is broadly predictable but not set in the early stages. It may be targeted in terms of time-scale or other hard criteria. Under conditions of high uncertainty, early milestones are set and revised using data from initial sorties. They are only set as far ahead as the team can reasonably see. Milestones only become fixed further ahead when the detailed ground becomes clear and when success or failure can be said to derive from the team's competence or inefficiency rather than from chance. Reaching frequent milestones along the route is a crucial part of the Superteam's motivational strategy which is built on people's need for success, for as everyone knows, success breeds success.

They also ensure that the team can never go too far off track. They are its early warning system, its insurance policy against failure before it's too late to correct.

Planning the What

Suggestions for Superteams

KEEP IT SIMPLE

Think about ways in which you can communicate The Big Picture simply and graphically on a regular basis. It should contain four main elements.

1. What we have achieved
   - highlight successes
   - set new milestones for those who are behind
2. What we are planning to achieve
   - show core activities and milestones. Try bar charts or graphs for simplicity.
3. Background information on context
   - identify what lies behind decisions, especially those coming from clients or sponsors.
4. How we're working as a team
   - celebrate outstanding performers highlight areas for improvement

Make it attractively presented, well written and keep the whole thing no longer than four pages. Remember — it is *your* responsibility to make people want to read it.

BRINGING PEOPLE TOGETHER

Where you find that there are several individuals in different departments or locations working on the same project, check to see if they are working with linear logic or parallel implementation.

If each is essentially working in isolation and then passing a completed bit over to the next person, *make them get together* to see if they can find ways to concertina the whole process. There will always be ways they can speed up what they're doing when they

65

look at the whole project in the round rather than from their narrow specialist viewpoint.

The same applies to getting planners and doers working together or all those involved in the development of the business or organisation. For example form joint teams between corporate planners, research and development and marketing. Bring together the customer, design and manufacturing. Get Merchandising, Buyers and Store Managers talking to each other. Bring doctors, administrators, patients and their families together.

MAKING COMPUTERS USER-FRIENDLY

The computer should be a slave. Don't let it become the master! Remember, *you* are the user and it should give you what you need.

Its two great advantages are its ability to do things quickly and its ability to handle huge amounts of detail. Go for the speed — that must be a vital asset for a team that wants to be responsive and adaptable. But don't get seduced into getting any more detail than you need. That will bog you down just when you need to react fast.

SEARCHING QUESTIONS

When Planning the What it is easy to get blind spots and only be able to see one way of scheduling activities. Superteams are always asking searching questions to help them 'break set' and stimulate creativity in order to see if there are better ways of doing things. Here are some examples.

- How could we do it faster, or more cheaply?
- Are we doing more than we need to?
- What can we routinise, standardise or automate?
- What causes hold-ups and how can they be avoided?
- Has excessive slack time been built into the plan?
- What operations can we cut out or reduce?
- What about doing things in a different order? Perhaps doing the last bit first.
- Could we learn from someone else to save time?

- How can we increase capacity and throughput: for example, subcontractors, outworkers, temporary staff, joint ventures.
- How would we need to change the design or specification to speed up manufacture or to simplify delivery, or to reduce development time?
- Are the constraints real or assumed? How could we overcome them?

BE CLEAR ABOUT WHAT YOU KNOW AND WHAT YOU DON'T KNOW

To avoid trying to plan the unplannable identify *Zones of Certainty* and *Zones of Uncertainty*.

Zones of Certainty

Where you have all the information and experience you need and can plan forward realistically.

Zones of Uncertainty

Where you are ignorant or where there is a great uncertainty, start *doing* things. Go and find out from people who might know the area; start some limited experiments or trials. Then feed that information into the team *quickly*, so that it can be used to plan forward a bit more and make decisions about what to do next.

7 Planning the how

If you talk to people who have been members of very good teams, they always communicate a sense of the excitement and intense commitment that they felt. One of their most frequently used phrases is 'the chemistry was right'. One of the most public examples we know is the team that made the humorous, anti-war television series MASH. In a film about the making of MASH, these are some of the things that they said about their team.

- 'It was a very personal show — a confluence of key people who translated their feelings about the world'
- '. . . a real sense of purpose has never been lost'
- '. . . real persistence — they believed in themselves . . . and had others in high places who believed in them.'
- 'All the members enjoy what they're doing and enjoy each other'
- 'Losing a key actor looked like a real threat to the series — but was turned into an opportunity. It changed the chemistry and helped us to generate a whole lot of new stories.'
- 'The organisation has become a community of mutual support — there is a desire to draw out of us all what we can contribute.'

At a recent World Congress on Project Management, at which one of us described our approach to developing Superteams, the following question was asked of the several hundred delegates:

'What is the most crucial area currently of interest to Project Management?'

A staggering 72.6 per cent said it was 'educating the Project Management team in the human aspects of Project Management'.

During this congress, one of the delegates, himself the leader of a large project team, described the issue as follows:

> 'We have all the hardware, the technical systems well developed. We are comfortable controlling technology and money and suchlike. But it's the software, the programming of the team . . . we don't think about how to programme the *human* system to perform as we want it to; all our attention goes on the technical aspects, and yet in our heart of hearts we know that they don't go right unless you also get the people factors right'

What the MASH team and this project manager were struggling to find words to express is what we refer to as Planning the How. It's not an easy concept initially because it seems so intangible.

One of the big mistakes of the past has been to work with the false assumptions that if a group of people are given a challenging and exciting enough job to do, success will follow. Not so. Superteams don't just happen, they are made to happen. Although many a team will engage in something akin to planning the how, the difference with the Superteam lies in its control and understanding of what it's doing. It knows that there are a number of important factors it has to get right if it is to create the environment where people give of their best.

Look back at those comments by the MASH team. They describe some of what it feels like to work in a Superteam. The MASH team almost certainly didn't sit down to plan formally — it just happened. Our idea of planning the how is not leave that to chance.

DEVELOPING GROUND RULES FOR SUCCESS

Another way of looking at Planning the How is to observe the results when it is absent. A client company sent a number of separate departmental heads on a programme intended to help them work and feel more like a team. They had been criticised by a new general manager because they didn't work closely enough together. They were a sullen and silent group at first. Gradually as they warmed up they started grumbling about the company and changes that were being made. They argued a lot with each other about trivial issues, avoided confronting serious ones, but were in general rather polite to one another. They were united in their opposition to the new General Manager in the company and were generally unenthusiastic and pessimistic about the future. They spent a lot of time reminiscing about the good old days. When finally one of us asked whether they considered themselves an effective team, the answer came back "of course; we've known each other for twenty years".

Somehow, the magic ingredient X was missing from this 'team'. And the saddest thing was they didn't even know it. Much of our work with them was to start them thinking about planning the how; to get them to discuss 'the way we do things round here' and to assess the impact of their unwritten ground rules most of which guaranteed mediocrity. Happily they began to see that there were some alternatives that would make them not only more productive as a team but also more satisfied as individuals. As our work with them progressed they began to change their outlook from that of a group that was cruising along, to that of a team that was speeding ahead. They began for the first time to begin to get control of the twin engines of success. The first being to create excitement about their purpose; *what* they were trying to achieve and *what* was expected of them, and the second looking at *how* they were to drive themselves forward and *how* they were to bind themselves together more closely.

The result of planning the how together is that the team is able to articulate in the broadest way some philosophies and rules about how individual members and the team as a whole are to work. Once talked through, these ground rules cease to be conscious — they become engraved on the minds of the leader and members and often those outside the team with whom they work. In the experienced team they become second nature and will only need to be referred to when they are violated or need to be changed. They become like the software programme that instructs the computer — invisible but powerful. Their hidden effect is to ensure that the behaviour of both insiders and outsiders supports and promotes rather than acts against the team and its purpose.

In the next three sections of this chapter, we explore some of the areas in which a team may need to develop ground rules as it embarks on Planning the How.

MANAGING THE OUTSIDE

In Chapter 5, 'Managing the Outside,' we stressed the importance of the team's image and credibility with outsiders. Managing these important external relationships well is one of the keys to develop a clear sense of the team's purpose and direction. It is also crucial in securing the right resources when they are required. The team will have a number of targets to think about and a number of questions that they will be posing to themselves.

The client or customer

What is the history of the relationship and how might that affect the current situation? What sort of people are involved as clients or end users? How good are we at empathising with them, really understanding and seeing their situation through *their* eyes? Who is going to handle the clients, how and when? How can the client help us?

The sponsor

Again, the effect of history may be an important factor to consider. What is the Sponsor's previous thinking and track record in relation to what the team is doing? Is the sponsor already committed or will he or she need to be persuaded? How influential credible and powerful is the sponsor? How good a network of relationships at the right level inside and outside the organisation does the sponsor have? What sort of style and approach is the Sponsor likely to respond positively to? What 'hidden agendas' or constraints might the sponsor have? How is the team going to keep the sponsor informed, and how often? How to get the sponsor on our side? How to use the sponsor's antennae in the organisation to pick up feedback about the team?

The organisation

Which are the key relationships? Who gains and loses as a result of what we are doing? How will we relate to the losers, or any others who might wish to undermine us, or are envious of us? What means will we use to communicate with the organisation? Who is going to do what and when?

All of these questions and many more will be asked not only about Clients, Sponsors and the organisation but about service departments, subcontractors and gatekeepers. The result of all the questioning and the discussions that follow, is that the Superteam develops a clear idea of the kinds of relationships with each of these outsiders that it feels will help it to achieve its task most successfully. The team emerges in effect with a comprehensive strategy for managing the outside, that is tailored to its situation and which provides clear guidelines to leader and members about how they should conduct themselves with outsiders, and what their objectives are in those relationships.

DRIVING IT FORWARD

Leaders and members of Superteams have abundant energy not because they are any different from anyone else, but because the Superteam environment is designed to release their enthusiasm and motivation. We use the word 'designed' deliberately — planning the how is about designing the human system by using a good understanding of what it is that makes people want to perform well.

Piling on the pressure

Superteam leaders and members are able to work under considerable pressure and indeed thrive on the adrenaline that this produces. They work long hours and make considerable personal sacrifices for the team. 'Why do they do that?' one might well ask. The answer is that there is something in it for them — they get out of it the satisfaction that they are looking for.

In Superteams there is a unique kind of 'psychological contract' between the individual and the team. It demands an exceptional level of personal commitment of time, skill and emotional energy in return for opportunity, satisfaction and rewards. These are a soft criteria that the leader needs to communicate to prospective team members before they join the team, because for some it may not be acceptable, and they may choose not to become involved.

This level of personal commitment does not, however, materialise just because the leader demands it. It comes because the Superteam plans how to earn it. It plans how to create the conditions in which its members will want to work under pressure, under which they will be setting their own high standards, and, through the team and its work, finding their own satisfactions.

So, once again, the team will be asking itself a number of questions about how it sustains the pressure. Is the vision itself sufficiently inspiring and challenging for the team? Are there some individuals who find it less than stretching? What about individual objectives and milestones — are they acting as positive motivators? How will the team handle the situation when some people are temporarily under or over worked? How do we handle people who appear to be coasting or underperforming? How is the team going to reward and celebrate success? What are the incentives to people to perform outstandingly? Answers to these sorts of questions provide the environment for the team leader and members to give the exceptional commitment that Superteams need.

Problems? What problems?

Superteams evolve powerful approaches and attitudes to confronting problems. A crucial part of their attitude is to see problems as normal. They don't let problems get them down. Indeed they make drama and excitement out of overcoming obstacles. Put quite simply solving problems and overcoming obstacles turns them on.

This intensely positive attitude can be overwhelming to outsiders or new members of the team, particularly if they don't understand the assumptions and rules that the team is working to. Defining these underlying assumptions and ground rules which make this positive problem-solving approach possible, is another component of planning the how. The ground rules make it clearer to all *why* the Superteam searches exhaustively for alternatives and creative ways of doing things. They make it clear why, when a decision has been made, it is acceptable to change it later because someone has found a better way. They make it clear why the phrase 'How to' is so much part of the Superteam vocabulary, which contains no such words as 'can't' or 'difficult'. Instead they will come back by saying 'how to . . .' or 'how can we . .' or 'what if . .'.

The individual contribution

Superteams paradoxically attract individualists, who see in the team a way of contributing their unique skills, developing their competence and confidence, while at the same time meeting the needs of the organisation.

Part of developing the ground rules concerns negotiating the balance between individual and team. In Superteams the balance is much further towards the individual because members are trusted and understand so much more about what is required of them and the team. The team in turn benefits from allowing greater autonomy and responsibility because that releases the individual's energy and commitment, and places less burden on the leader to get involved in operational detail.

Part of planning the how, therefore, is to try to ensure all the energy skills and experience that individuals bring to the team are fully utilised. And that will encompass far more than will just their specialist knowledge.

One of us worked with a task group in a small electronics company. They had been asked by the board to make recommendations about how the company should structure itself in the future. At first they decided they knew little about structures. However, they decided to carry out an audit of members' background experience, employment history, general interests and key contacts. They found to their surprise that they had between them enormous direct experience of different structures in different organisations and access to people with expertise in restructuring organisations.

Allowing scope for individuals to contribute widely and in so doing to develop and extend their competences is very much something that Superteams value and plan for because they realise how much it can contribute to individual motivation. Likewise, they plan for the flexibility in roles which encourages and demands of people that they extend themselves, and contribute to and learn from the problems of the other team members.

BINDING IT TOGETHER

Because Superteams are often made up of individuals; because they all work under intense pressure, and because they are frequently working apart, Superteams are inherently unstable and fragile. They have an inbuilt tendency to self destruct!

It is because they recognise these extreme dangers to their success and survival that they take strong measures to ensure that the whole fabric of the team holds together. They will do this by developing ground rules which cover four important areas, helping people to belong, togetherness, support and communication. These four activities, when carried out with the Superteams skill and attention to detail, are the glue that binds the team together.

Helping people to belong

We can still see the rueful face of one new team member who had recently joined a very busy project team. She described how when she arrived no-one knew she was coming and initially there was no desk for her to sit at. Her new boss was on holiday and on his return spent only a brief time welcoming her before giving her her first assignment. She knew little of the project's background nor precisely where her role fitted in. Neither did she know other specialists in the project to whom she should refer. Of course in time she picked this all up but only in a haphazard way. And for a long time she was less efficient than she might have been, not to mention having feelings of loneliness and resentment.

What she should have had was a properly thought out induction process — not an empty formality but a vital process to integrate her quickly into the team. This should have covered an explanation of the Big Picture, her role and performance expectations, some of the team's more important ground rules, and introductions to her key internal and external contacts. In addition her colleagues should have been quick to ask her about her own background and skills to see the best ways in which she could make her contribution.

Togetherness

Apart from planning how to bring new people into the team, the Superteam will be thinking about how they can create a sense of identity for the team, what one of our clients calls the 'we feeling'. This becomes of particular importance if the team is dispersed.

The team will therefore plan how often it is going to come together recognising its symbolic importance. But Superteams will go a lot further than this. For them working hard and living hard is a way of life. Work and leisure merge. Leader and members are often found having impromptu social get togethers especially when the going has been tough for a while. Even these serve the purpose of work. Work is fun and fun is work. Superteams always talk shop and get immense satisfaction from it. They find attractive ways of being together.

Support

An essential ground rule for Superteams is that the team leader and team members send out early warning signals if they are experiencing problems. Everyone is encouraged to ask for support. The team needs to feel confident about this particular rule, because there is a natural inhibition, especially amongst people who drive themselves hard or are individualists, about asking for help. They will therefore legitimise it by talking about it. They will also identify some of the factors that should trigger calls for help as well as exploring a range of simple ways in which support can be offered to others.

Communication

The Superteam's internal communications are the single most important factor in building it together for they are at the heart of its ability to respond quickly, to change and to stay flexible. They form the team's nervous system which coordinates the movement of all its diverse activities, but they also fuel the teams cohesiveness and sense of belonging.

Planning how to communicate with each other while under pressure, and especially when the team is apart becomes a regular preoccupation. It is so central that it forms an important element in the leader's role to be constantly monitoring and easing the flow of information. However, members bear equal responsibility for initiating and monitoring communication: the leader cannot do it alone.

A whole range of issues will therefore confront the team as it thinks about communication. For instance, who has information and who needs it? How best can we stay in touch, keep ourselves updated? What formal methods can we use — letters, reports, notice boards, briefing groups information systems, review meetings and suchlike. What informal methods are worth pursuing — such as impromptu small meetings, telephone calls, social activities or bringing the coffee machine nearer!

Superteams capitalise fully on all the available formal and informal ways of keeping each in touch. But above all their preference is for the speed and pleasure of informal person-to-person communication. They like talking to each other, and they find opportunities to do it a lot, recognising that this personal contact, above all else, cements the relationships within the team, and that in turn ensures that communication is open, two-way, fast and accurate.

CHANGING THE RULES

Perhaps the final and most important part of planning the how is not in setting the ground rules but in knowing when to change them. If the rules, be they explicit or unwritten, are not helping the team to achieve its results, then they need looking at. It is a fact of life that situations change. Superteams assume constant change, and are therefore always on the look out to see whether they need to alter the way they do things.

That is why we like the quote at the head of this chapter, for in some ways it sums up the Superteam attitude. But in others, it is not right because there *are* some golden rules, which we have explored above, which apply to all team situations at all times. Planning the how is about making sure that the team applies them.

Planning the How

Suggestions for Superteams

EARLY WARNING SYSTEMS

How often in your team do you get unexpected (nasty) surprises, when problems suddenly come from nowhere?

This is an indication that there is no ground rule about anticipating, looking ahead and then signalling problems as soon as they appear over the horizon. When they hit you, it's too late.

What is stopping people from signalling problems? And what can you do about it?

TIME-OUTS

Ensure that your team finds time regularly to review *not what* it is doing, but *how* it is working. Identify the written and unwritten ground rules and check that they are working for the team rather than against it.

If you have a new team in particular, take them away from the workplace, perhaps with a teamworking consultant to help, and spend time exclusively on designing the kind of team you need to be in order to achieve your task successfully. Ask yourselves in particular how you as a team will handle some specific situations or events that might prove especially difficult.

SOMEONE AT THE CENTRE

Ideally every team should have someone at its centre who draws in, and re-routes information. Secretaries are a much underutilised resource in this respect. Help them to belong to the team at an early stage, let them understand the Big Picture and all other aspects of the team's work. They will then be in a unique position to be thinking about and monitoring the efficiency of the team's communications.

IMPROMPTU GET TOGETHERS

Don't adopt the idea that the only time the team gets together is for formal scheduled meetings. Try to find as many opportunities as possible for people to work together and to talk over work issues together. Get the team enjoying themselves together. Encourage people to bounce ideas off each other or seek each others opinion and advice. Have a convenient place where team members bump into each other regularly such as a notice board, or post room or coffee machines.

COMMUNICATING THE VISION

Think about how best to get people excited and enthused about the vision. Consider doing it with a bit of drama, build up and flair, as if you were launching a revolutionary new product or service onto the market.

THE TEAM PHOTO

You may want to do it like the old school photograph. But consider an alternative. On a large board draw a picture or organigram showing the relationship of people in your team and also important members of your invisible team. Put a picture of each person with their role and name in the appropriate place, and put this somewhere public.

Incidentally — if you opt for the traditional version, how about inviting the invisible team too?

---

8 Leading the team

'Leading a team is like juggling with eggs. You have to keep them all on the move simultaneously, and if you drop one you end up with a nasty mess'

Anonymous programme participant

Jan Versluys was a very good research biotechnologist working in the development laboratories of an international food group. Jan was appointed leader of a small multidisciplinary team of eight people, responsible for developing a new food product. He had been used to working a lot on his own and controlling his own time. Suddenly he found himself being pulled in all directions as demands were made on him by his team's sponsor, by the group company that was the client, and by members of his team. He was frustrated by not being able to get on with what he saw as his important contribution to some of the technical aspects of how the product was to be made. He was inexperienced and lacked confidence in handling all the relationships that suddenly became important and couldn't understand the apparent hostility he sometimes received from his team members. As the project slipped behind schedule Jan became increasingly withdrawn and preoccupied.

Jan's predicament was spotted by his sponsor, an experienced team leader, who helped him over time to understand his new team leader role, and in particular how it was different from his previous technical role. While he still required a technical understanding of what team members were doing, he did not need to get involved in the detail. The new part of his role was to let go of that and to manage and motivate others to do it. 'Your job' said his sponsor, 'is to create an environment which stimulates team members and your invisible team to perform outstandingly. Your job is also to be looking in a number of other directions simultaneously, switching your attention frequently across a wide range of problems and issues that affect the team's performance'.

Jan learned from his mistakes. He also learned from others when his organisation nominated him for a systematic team leader development programme run by outside consultants. He discovered that he must look forward by planning and providing direction for his team. He began to enjoy looking outside his team to build its credibility and secure resources. He learned to look inside at how his team was working and ways that it could be improved, and he became increasingly confident in being able to talk with individual team members about their performance. The rest of this chapter examines each of these elements in greater detail.

LOOKING FORWARDS

The leaders of Superteams spend as much time anticipating the future as they do managing the present. This is not to say that they spend half their time in detailed planning though that will be part of it. It is more that they devote time to thinking forward to, and talking to others about, their goal, for it is this that provides the team with its purpose and direction.

What are we here for?

Leaders of Superteams are good at creating visions. Visions in this sense are not the vague, mystical or unrealistic products of the wandering mind. They are instead vivid pictures of what the team is trying to achieve. The vision is a statement of where the team is heading and what it stands for. Its purpose is to create challenge and excitement and a common direction for the teams activities.

A vision can exist at a number of different levels. Bob Geldof, founder of Live Aid, brought together a team that created a global rock show seen by 1500 million people and which raised over £50m for famine relief. 'Our concerts are trying to keep the starving alive' he said, 'now let us give them a life'. At a different level, an aircraft production team one of us was working with developed a vision of how they could totally reorganise their production and office layouts to improve productivity and teamwork. Given the enthusiasm and the potential benefits they saw in the ideas, nothing could stop this team from achieving their goal.

Leaders of Superteams are especially good at drawing out what is unique or special about either their team's goal or how it will be accomplished. People develop pride and commitment through their association with an exciting objective. If leaders and team members together can be involved in developing the vision themselves, then its power to motivate is further enhanced.

Anticipating

We have found that Superteam leaders have a very important quality in greater measure than leaders of ordinary teams. And that is their ability to think forward and anticipate events. It is as if they constantly send out radar signals which bounce back from the team's objective enabling the leader to measure the distance and the obstacles between where the team is currently and where it wants to be.

Linked to this is their ability to make quick and almost intuitive, but realistic, estimates of the implications of what they see. This enables them to re-plan rapidly with the team and to redirect resource and effort as appropriate to ensure they reach their objective.

Creating the climate for success

In a large financial institution, the Chief Executive had set the organisation the task of becoming more innovative. The requirement was for the top team members to find new and creative ways of streamlining paperwork and bureaucratic procedures, as well as to find new products that met the needs of a rapidly changing market. In this organisation, which had set ways of doing things and which had not undergone much change for many years, finding new ways of working involved an element of risk. Initially, the objectives created excitement and released some new energy. However very soon, instead of people trying out new approaches, the Chief Executive found that team members were reverting to the old ways.

On closer examination, consultants found that, while the leader had invited innovation, creativity, and risk taking, as soon as someone made a mistake, they were penalised or punished in some way by the Chief Executive. The climate he had created through his behaviour led his team members in the opposite direction to that he had intended.

There are a number of ways in which leaders can contribute to creating a positive climate within a team.

- First, as we've outlined above, they can *put forward an exciting vision* of what the team is to achieve, and they can with equal skill and enthusiasm 'sell' this to the rest of the organisation just as much as to the team itself.

- Secondly, where possible, they may be able to select or *influence the composition of the team*. It helps to have team members who are turned on by the vision — some may not be. It also helps to select people who themselves have outstanding membership attributes and qualities.

- Thirdly, as we have said in the previous chapter on Planning the How, leaders of Superteams will spend significant time with their teams *talking about what sort of climate and ways of working together are likely to contribute to their joint success*. A well understood set of principles, developed together by the leader and the team, creates a favourable climate.

- Fourthly, they can lay the foundations for the team's success by *contracting skilfully* with the sponsor, the client and service departments. The result should be a clear definition of the team's parameters and the full commitment of the invisible team to its success.

- Fifthly, and we believe most importantly, leaders *create the climate within a team through their own behaviour and attitudes*. Superteam leaders, therefore, are very aware of how they appear to others. They are also clear about what kinds of qualities and values they need to demonstrate through their own behaviour in order to set standards, communicate what they expect, and inspire their team members to do likewise.

There is a range of such qualities and values which we associate in particular with Superteam leaders, and which set them apart from the leaders of ordinary teams. They start by having a strong belief in the vision and an unshakeable confidence and trust that their team will realise that vision. They have a great enthusiasm, positiveness and persistence — they don't ever use the word 'failure' — they only see problems or setbacks as challenges to be overcome. This overiding optimism is tempered by toughness and realism. They are enormously demanding of themselves and of others, communicating at times great impatience and sense of urgency. They appraise situations thoroughly and are not afraid to confront facts that are uncomfortable. But even when times are bad they remain approachable, open to ideas and supportive of their team.

MANAGING TEAM MEMBERS' PERFORMANCE

We have come across a belief amongst team leaders in many organisations that all they have to do to get results is tell people what needs doing. This is particularly so amongst teams of technical specialists who tend to feel that the technical specification, together with some deadlines, guarantees good performance from team members. This *laissez-faire* style of team leadership leads to no more than average results.

In contrast, roles, objectives and performance standards are constantly talked about in Superteams and are regularly agreed and monitored jointly by the leader and the members. The leaders of Superteams take a dynamic role in helping others to perform. They demonstrate to their team members that they are motivated by high quality and high standards and they relish the pride and satisfaction that these bring. They also realise that high performance doesn't just happen — it must be planned for.

Communicating performance expectations

The process starts with the team as a whole coming to understand their success criteria fully. Sometimes they all hear these from the clients, customers or sponsor. More often though they hear them second hand through the leader and perhaps other team members who have been talking to the customer. We have found repeatedly that success criteria from outside are either not heard, not recorded or not communicated accurately to the team. In particular technical specialists find it difficult to pick up and convey the flavour of the client's soft criteria which, though intangible, are often crucial.

The next step for the leader is to translate the overall team's success criteria into success criteria for each team member. Apart from understanding the general aspects of their role, team members should also be given specific objectives to achieve within specified timeframes. These will often coincide with key milestones in a team's activities. However, if the milestones are far apart, the objective should be broken down into smaller elements or 'stepping stones'.

However, defining objectives is not enough. There needs to be agreement between the leader and each member on both the hard and soft criteria of performance and how their performance is to be judged.

These discussions form the unwritten 'contract' between leaders and members. Not only do the members agree their contribution, measures and objectives, but the team leader also agrees how he or she can help (or avoid hindering) the team members' achievements.

One team member was feeling very pleased with herself when she devised at very short notice some highly innovative designs for the racking and layout in a new store. She was then rightly dismayed when the project team leader told her they were no good because their cost exceeded the reduced budget that had recently been agreed. Her speed of response and creativity were soft performance criteria that should have been appreciated, but the hard criteria of revised budget limits was not communicated to her.

Another team member delivered some prototype components to a team meeting on time. He was surprised by the cool reaction he got from one of his colleagues. It turned out that he had hijacked one of his colleague's specialist staff to help him without asking the colleague. The result was that the colleague had missed his deadline! The team leader and his colleagues very quickly showed him the error of his ways.

Keeping performance on track

In Superteams, team members discuss and monitor progress frequently with the leader. This process is important because it provides a regular sense of success and achievement as the work progresses. It also provides quick and regular feedback for the leader to spot problems and put them right. A Superteam member seldom fails to reach a milestone because problems are anticipated early. Leaders of Superteams believe that it's bad for the individual to fail. It's bad for the team because when the milestone is missed it's too late to correct. It's bad for the leader whose credibility suffers by either not being aware of a problem or not taking appropriate action soon enough. And it's bad for the individual who loses confidence.

The whole workings of a Superteam are built on rapid and honest feedback about what is happening. The leader's contribution to this process is to create the environment where team members will feel free to say what they see and foresee as well as what they feel or think. For the fast flow of the sort of information provides the vital early warning system that the leader needs to take corrective action.

Hands on or hands off

A characteristic of many new types of teams is that they are made up of different specialists who are bright and intelligent and like their independence. By nature they are not always the most natural teamworkers!

Managing these people's performance presents the team leader with a delicate balancing act between the hands on and the hands off approach.

The hands on approach takes an active interest on a very regular basis in the members work. If the level is not right it is seen as interfering or anxious. Where a high level of hands on is appropriate is early in the team's life when definitions are still being agreed. Likewise it is appropriate when someone is new or inexperienced in a role or when performance is continuously below standard. In this last situation the leader has to move in fast and find out why.

The hands off approach trusts team members and recognises their needs for autonomy to carry out their role as they see fit. It trades on their self motivation. If it goes too far on the other hand, the leader is seen as abdicating or not being interested.

Celebrating success

One other simple way in which Superteams' leaders manage performance is by talking to many different people about times when the team or particular individuals excelled. They celebrate successes and publicise them widely. These stories are relished (and probably embellished) but they serve a very important function. They provide vivid pictures, models and examples for team members of the kinds of performance to strive for. They express the teams' internal standards of excellence about the way they want to work. But having the performance made public is also a way of providing reward in the form of recognition to good performers. Being approached in the corridor by a colleague or sponsor saying, 'I heard about what you did — it sounds fantastic' is a potent stimulus to the team member to keep up the good work. Superteams' leaders enjoy the successes of their team.

Each individual responds in different ways. Which style to use is a product of experience but also the ability to observe closely and find out about the particular team member's reactions and motivations.

LOOKING INWARDS

Having agreed standards of performance for individuals and the team as a whole, the leader's role is then to act as the guardian of those standards. In ordinary teams the issue is seldom discussed and hence the leader tends to spend considerable time on technical matters. For the Superteam leader, however, the guardianship becomes a significant part of the role. And it involves a rather special quality which leaders of ordinary teams may lack.

The Helicopter view

The quality we refer to is known as the Helicopter quality. It was first identified by researchers in Shell who found that it was the only consistent factor that distinguished all their more effective managers from their less effective managers.

The Helicopter quality is the ability to rise above day-to-day events and pressures and to take a broader and more objective view of what is going on and what is likely to happen. It is like taking an aerial snapshot looking inside the team. It provides the leader with a bigger picture of what is happening. In simple terms its the ability to be able to 'see the wood from the trees'.

A machine tool company had recently taken over a small company that specialised in electronics control systems. A project team was assembled from both the companies to put the two technologies together and create a new generation of electronically controlled machine tools.

The project was beset with technical problems with all parties regularly late on milestones and the project manager firefighting continuously. It was only when the project manager went on holiday and had time to reflect that the truth dawned. The real problem was a total clash of attitudes and approach between the way things were done in the two companies. The old fashioned machine tool company was solid, systematic and bureaucratic; the electronics company intuitive, quick with decisions and a bit disorganised. Taking the helicopter view helped the team leader to reframe the problem — to see that it was about distrust, suspicion and wariness between two different approaches rather than just about technical problems. It was only when the project manager was able to take the helicopter view that the problems could be clearly seen.

One word of warning though to leaders who helicopter and then swoop in to sort problems out. Beware of the seagull syndrome! The European Division of an American multinational had its boss in the parent company based in New York. When he left the job to move on in the company, he was presented with a giant plastic blow-up seagull. When he asked about the particular significance of the present he was told smilingly, 'When you come from New York for one of your quick visits, you're just like a seagull. You fly in, circle round, make a lot of noise, shit on a few people and fly off again!'

The Big Picture seen by helicoptering should be communicated on a regular basis by the team leader to team members. It provides them with a progress report on the what and the how. It looks forward in outline and anticipates problems before they occur. It provides regular milestones for each team member to be working towards, and it shows team members how their roles fit into the whole and how they integrate with each other.

Being able to take the helicopter view is a vital skill for the leader who wants to look inside the workings of the team and monitor what is going on. Occasionally then the leader will swoop down on to the ground to take a more detailed look at some aspect of the situation with the team or a particular member and perhaps take corrective action. Leaders will monitor progress in this way both on what is happening and on how it is being performed. Through helicoptering too, the leader will be able to identify changes in the team's situation which perhaps requires new or amended ground rules about how the team should be working. Superteam leaders are constantly moving up and down, in and out in this way, moving from the general to the detail and back again.

Holding it all together

There are a number of forces and factors that can have the effect of splitting a team apart and it is the team leader's responsibility to hold it together as long as it still has a job to do.

Clashes of personality or competition between vested interests within the team can have a debilitating splintering effect. In the main Board of a firm distributing agricultural machinery, the financial director and after-sales directors used to have bitter confrontations at almost every meeting while the rest of the Board either took sides or sat by as bemused spectators. These confrontations diverted energy away from the Board's main business and had a serious effect on the morale of other members, as well as on co-operation between the two departments lower down the organisation.

Neither the managing director nor outside consultants were able to make any impact on the problem — it had run too deep for too long — and it was only solved when the managing director engineered the transfer of the after-sales director to another subsidiary.

Even without such dramatic happenings, meetings of teams can fall apart in disorganisation and confusion with everyone talking simultaneously. In a Superteam, the leader will take some of the responsibility for introducing order and discipline but will also expect team members to share that responsibility.

However, the most serious form of splitting that faces many modern times is that of the physical separation of its members. For some such as Sales teams or teams in transport industries, having the members of the team in dispersed locations has long been a way of life. But for others it is new. We have devoted a whole chapter of this book (Chapter 11) to managing 'the team apart' because we believe it is a neglected and little understood aspect of teamworking.

The leader's role when team members are dispersed is particularly crucial. For what often happens is that the team loses its identity and cohesion at such times. The leader must be particularly sensitive to the needs of distant sites which often feel out of touch and neglected. Ways must be found of keeping these members updated and involved. Modern methods of communication help considerably, but even so the project manager of one of the North Sea gas teams that we have worked with, which had team members in six different locations hundreds of miles apart insisted that the whole team must meet together at least once every six weeks. He said he did this for three reasons. First he found that the project, despite detailed and agreed schedules, would start to slide off track because letters, computers and telephones could not produce a common understanding amongst team members of what was and was not happening. Only face to face meetings could do this complex job efficiently. Second, he found that misunderstandings and misperceptions started to escalate over time unless clarified by face to face meetings. And thirdly, he found that the meetings, often two days in length so that members could spend time socially together as well, were important to rebuild the togetherness, the sense of common identity, and the cohesion of the team. Without this sense, team members felt isolated and lost much of the feeling of strength and support that comes from belonging to a Superteam.

LOOKING OUTWARDS

More than any single person in the team, it is the leader's role to manage the outside. The leader is the bridge that connects the outside to the inside, supplemented in the Superteam by the bridges that members build. An important part of the leader's role is to ensure that the flow of information, resources and support is a two-way traffic, inside–out and outside–in.

Inside–Out

Outsiders need to know about the team's project just as much as the team itself. Sponsors need to know whether the team is reaching the organisation's objectives and to be given honest and realistic information. A small team starting a new up-market shop for a confectionery company, consistently gave their sponsor sales forecasts which they didn't meet. They kept on maintaining that 'next month' the market would pick up. In truth the shop was wrongly sited and they couldn't admit to themselves or to the sponsor that this was the case. The leader had to accept the responsibility for avoiding the issue. Leaders and teams lose credit very quickly through this type of behaviour.

The leader should also ensure all team members are giving consistent messages to the outside. Any confusion inside the team is quickly transmitted and amplified within the organisation or subcontractors. And once misunderstandings occur, they are often time consuming to unravel.

The leader also has an important role in sanctioning and encouraging at times a blurring of the boundaries between inside and outside in order to encourage teamworking. This usually takes the form of inviting members of the invisible team to put at least one foot in the team camp. For instance we have regularly seen team members and their subcontractors sharing open plan offices, or at least brought together in the same building. Or conversely, the leader will ask a team member to have a linking role with a particular department and to be located in that department on a full or part time basis.

Outside–In

If the leader's preparation has been well done, the connections built up, the relationships developed and the commitment secured, then information resource and support from the outside should flow steadily.

It is when the flow stops for some reason that team members may need the support of their leader. The leader may have to involve the sponsor or a service department head for instance in discussion to resolve the issue.

On a more positive note, Superteam leaders realise the power of bringing important outsiders to visit the team as a way of spurring motivation. Inviting clients' sponsors, service department heads and other members of senior management to inspect the team's work has important symbolic and motivational benefits for both sides.

Protecting the team

One final and useful function that the leaders can perform is at times to protect the team from the demands or attacks of the outside. This is particularly important for teams facing very uncertain situations or for teams facing crises. At these times the members' full concentration needs to be on getting the job done and distractions from outside can impair performance. The Superteam leader in these circumstances, draws away the pressure from members.

Leading a Team
Suggestions for Superteams

HELPING OTHERS TO PERFORM

Team leaders should sit down on a regular basis with team members to talk about performance, especially with newer or less experienced people. Here are some simple questions that can be useful in the process.

- How do you see the key elements of your role?
- How will you know you've done each element well (hard and soft criteria)?
- Let's talk about key objectives during the next period.
- In what ways might I, other team members and outsiders, either help or hinder your performance?
- What actions does each need to take?

After your discussion, get the team members to summarise, in writing, their understanding of what they think has been agreed between you. This checks for any misunderstanding and serves as a useful checklist for subsequent monitoring.

PUBLISH YOUR VISION

For many leaders, finding a way of communicating their vision of the team can be problematic. Not all are good at public speaking. For these it may be more comfortable to do it in written or visual form. Here are some alternatives.

- Try to write down what you find exciting, stimulating and inspiring about the team's work. Allow yourself to wax lyrical if that's how you feel.

- Draw a diagram, picture or cartoon that expresses the Vision both in terms of what the team has to achieve and the kind of team it needs to be to achieve it.

You may well get invaluable help by involving team members in the process. This will help to share and cement the vision. Once completed, make sure it's widely seen either in report form or perhaps as posters for offices, stickers for cars or slogans for team letterheads and other communications.

PASSING THE BATON

Leaders can get stuck in their roles. Remember to exercise your power to do things differently. In particular, make demands of team members to help you out at times. Don't reinforce their expectations of you as a superhero; that's the first step towards a nervous breakdown. For instance:

- Ask a team member to take over chairing a meeting if you particularly want to contribute to the discussion and are finding it difficult to do both.
- Be prepared to say you don't know or don't understand.

HELPING YOURSELF TO PERFORM

Leading can be a lonely business. Who looks after leaders and their performance? The answer is that they often have to look after themselves. There are, however, some simple steps that you, the leader, can take.

- Use your sponsor: ensure that you sit down together to review your success criteria and how you are doing.
- Encourage frank feedback from others: ask others at all levels from time to time how they see you and your performance, and how they think you could improve.
- Develop a support network: get together with other leaders formally or informally to discuss common problems.

- Monitor your stress levels; realise when stress is having an adverse effect and do something about it. Look after yourself by eating and drinking sensibly and keeping fit.
- Using the summaries on pages 12 to 15, monitor your own performance in each area and set yourself goals for improvement.

REWARDING SUCCESS

One of the most potent motivational cards that leaders can play is to use the weight of their authority to give reward and recognition to those who have done particularly well. You can have a profound effect in a number of very simple ways.

- Send a personal, handwritten note offering congratulations and thanks.
- Talk or write publicly about people who are outstanding, describing what they did and why they were so successful.
- Hold parties and get-togethers to celebrate successes.
- Say 'well done' and 'thank you' to people's faces.

---

9 Membership

You need to surround yourself with able people who argue back
John Beckett, Chairman, Woolworths Holdings

Being a good team member is *not just* doing what's asked of you in the time allowed
Anonymous programme participant

This chapter is about team members and what makes the difference between the acceptable ones and the outstanding ones. The members are the lifeblood of the team, its most important resource. They bring different knowledge, competences and experience. And in Superteams they contribute these with enormous commitment, energy and enthusiasm. But we have found that outstandingly high performers bring more than their specialist knowledge to the team. They contribute a much wider range of acquired know-how and inbuilt qualities many of them paradoxically opposites which they balance and apply with fluid ease. In watching and working with these top team members, we have found that their actions and attitudes challenge some widely held beliefs about the effective team member. Let's take a close look at some of these beliefs together.

BELIEFS ABOUT LEADERS

'It's the leader's job to lead' is a statement that we often hear from team members. Who can dispute such a statement? But let's not accept it at face value because it often obscures a set of attitudes that poor team members have towards leaders.

One team member, for instance, used such a statement to justify his very passive role in the team, throwing much of the responsibility for the team's performance on to the leader and watching somewhat smugly as the leader sank under the weight of his expectations. Another team member used it aggressively against a leader whose role and authority she resented.

Both these team members revealed their own attitudes by pushing all the responsibility for the situation away from themselves and onto the leader. The result is a relationship between member and leader that is wary and antagonistic. Faced with hostility the leader may either fight it out or back off. Both strategies are damaging for the team because communication suffers, and members are likely to withhold crucial information. Superteam members on the other hand are more positive. They are able to give unequivocal support to the leader and others when they need it or ask for it. They are aware of what the leader requires. The relationship is relaxed but recognises the reality that the members are expected to perform. The leader tells the members what they want to know and in return good team members are alive to the leader's need for information on successful progress, current problems and early warning signals of issues over the horizon. In short the team member is thinking, anticipating and showing responsibility for the overall success of the team.

Another particular example of members avoiding their responsibility is where they insist that it is solely the chairman's job to manage meetings in an orderly manner. So it is in ordinary teams. But in Superteams members have greater skill in watching their own and other's behaviour. They do not rely solely on the discipline provided by the chairman. They provide their own internal self discipline and in so doing they free the leader to make a real contribution. In this sense the leader and members share the responsibility for how the team is working together.

BELIEFS ABOUT FOLLOWERSHIP

Children worldwide play the game 'Follow my Leader'. The concept of followership in this game is a passive one. The children follow the leader unquestioningly. There are of course powerful historical examples of followers demonstrating blind obedience and loyalty to a leader. While in organisations in the Western World there is seldom anything so extreme, we do often come across a tendency towards this passivity in certain team members who see their contribution as 'not stirring things up' or 'going along with the others'. Whilst it is a crucial skill of the team member to know when *not* to contribute and when to compromise, we cannot be satisfied with the team member who makes a purely passive contribution.

A team of six managers in a European subsidiary of an American pharmaceutical company were discussing a production reorganisation they were all involved in with their boss. Two of the managers stayed silent virtually throughout the meeting. When one of us asked them afterwards about their silence the first smiled and said, 'I'm entirely happy and committed to the proposals. I stayed quiet because it seemed the most helpful way to allow the other disagreements to be resolved'.

The point we made to her was that the weight of a simple statement of support for the proposals could have actually helped resolve some of the disagreement by persuading others to see its advantages. The second one responded resentfully that he disagreed with some elements of the plan but that there was 'no point in putting forward my concerns because no one would listen to me, so I just went along with it'. This resigned attitude helps no one, least of all the individual concerned. He and the rest of the team needed to find a way of airing and resolving the issues.

In Superteams, all members are active contributors and initiators. Members understand well how they can contribute both to what the team is doing and how it is going about doing it. In the extreme of course this becomes a recipe for anarchy or dominance by the few. What outstanding team members possess is the ability to be *active followers*. They know when to be in on the action and when to pull out. They know when to give help and when to ask for help. At times they will provide push and direction but equally they are able to allow themselves to be pulled by others. Their willingness to follow does not come from the passive obedience to the leader or others, but from their active loyalty, respect and personal commitment to all the members of the team. They are willing to be led by any of the team members provided that they can be persuaded that it is in the best interests of the team as a whole. But above all they assume responsibility. They take it upon themselves for instance to ensure that they understand how their role affects other peoples roles. They are driven by a desire not to let other people down, and when, as can always happen, this looks likely they take active steps to help their colleagues avoid or minimise the consequent problems. A reporter on a daily newspaper was sent far from base to cover an important story for the next day's edition. En route she fell, sustained mild concussion and had to be taken to hospital. Despite this she persuaded the hospital administrator to phone her editor to explain, and she managed to alert a local journalist she knew to cover the story. He brought the details to her in hospital so they could file a joint story that same afternoon. Active followers break the bad news — *before* it's too late!

BELIEFS ABOUT SPECIALISTS

We live in an age of specialism. Some of the phenomenal growth in the use of teams in organisations derives from the need to bring different specialists together. An underlying objective in multidisciplinary teams is to bring the combined brain power and differing perspectives of specialists to bear on a complex problem. That's the theory and when it works it's magnificent. But those very specialisms provide problems for teams because the members' attitudes to their own and other specialisms often prevent the team from performing to its full potential.

In the technical division of one airline, where there were many specialist departments, one engineer confessed that he often had no idea what some of the other technical specialists were saying in meetings and memos because of the string of jargon and acronyms that they used. Several others then confessed to the same problem and said that they just used to 'switch off' when people from certain departments started talking. Little wonder that the company had teamworking problems!

In a large hotel group we had long discussions about the inability and reluctance of their computer programmers and systems analysts to relate to the people who were going to use their systems. We stress the importance of designers and users seeing themselves as a team and working together at all stages. In Superteams the members who are technical specialists value their contacts with other specialists and those who use their services. Not only that, they go out and talk to people. They have the skills to develop relationships and build mutual respect and confidence by translating and explaining their specialism to others. They are also eager to find out in broad terms the expertise that other specialists have to offer. They see all the other specialists in their team not as boffins or blockages, but as resources that may help them or the team to do the job better. These members' attitude is to 'find out — not keep out'. When they don't understand they ask. Members of Superteams have no fear of looking foolish if they don't know because they recognise that they all need to learn from and value each other if the team is to benefit from its diversity of talent.

One final point about specialist members of teams; getting the right mix of specialisms is important to the team's success. But people putting together teams need to remember that technical specialisms alone are not enough for success. The members also need some of the teamworking skills and attributes that are described in this book to help them work in a team. When selecting members, their ability to contribute to the workings of the team needs to be considered just as much as their specialist technical skills. Likewise, technically brilliant specialists who are loners and introverts should not be promoted into core team membership or leadership. It is so often a recipe for misery both for them and those they struggle to manage. Better to leave them to progress and gain rewards for their technical achievement and let the core team use their expertise when it's needed.

BELIEFS ABOUT ROLES

Each member in a team usually has a role, which is a broad description of what that team is expected to do. The great danger about roles from the member's point of view is that they can become rigid and actually prevent achievement. The most extreme examples of this perhaps are restrictive practices. If members become trapped by their roles the team suffers. But so do individual team members because their development and initiative become stunted.

Superteam members avoid these rigid distinctions. They ensure their roles are described in general terms but not in such detail as to inhibit them. The core of the role is defined but the outer edges are left deliberately flexible and blurred. All the team members share the responsibility for keeping an eye open for potential problem areas. In many cases if they spot something that needs doing, they simply get on with it. If they cannot for any reason, they draw it to the attention of the team and it is quickly allocated to the person with time, interest or expertise. Members stick to their roles but also see the wider picture. The roles are part fixed and part flexible. For Superteam members there is no such phrase as, 'it's not my job'. Roles are not sacred — the main concern is for what needs doing and who is available and able to do it. As we've already said, Superteams recognise the significant work involved in helping the team to work better (and *how* of teamworking) and that this is a joint responsibility of leader and members. Furthermore, part of working better is to recognise when current roles no longer work and to make rapid adjustments. In one local government agency we worked with, the senior team realised the need to redefine the roles of its members as the agency's priorities and programmes changed. This in turn required a restructuring and redeployment of people into new teams within the organisation in order to achieve the new success criteria.

BELIEFS ABOUT CO-OPERATION

'Teamworking isn't natural' said one very frustrated team leader after a period when members of her team had been spending a lot of energy undermining each other. She was exasperated because some members seemed more intent going their own way or winning their own battles at the expense of others rather than pushing the team forward in the direction she thought it ought to go!

On the face of it both competitiveness and individualism are threats to teamworking. Colleagues can be seen as problems or rivals. And in some measure this is of course so. In Superteams however, there seems to be a willingness to preserve the energy, the dedication, the sacrifice and the desire to achieve that often comes with individualism and competitiveness. At the same time however they contain any possible damaging effects through clear ground rules and skills for maintaining open communication and resolving differences. When members of the team are working apart in particular, they may tend to forget they are still part of a team. Outstanding members, even though they may be individualists at heart, pay great attention to updating themselves on what's happening and ensure that they keep others informed too. They don't take the easy way out which is not to bother to communicate what they are doing and hope that others will discover eventually. These same members, when faced with direct conflicts with others will argue the merits of their case forcefully, but will also work hard at understanding the opposite case fully and will then join the team's search for a solution that meets the needs of both parties. Of course this is not always possible. In this case the 'winner' does not gloat and the 'loser' does not sulk. They move on because the decision was taken in the light of what was best for the team and not for the individuals.

The Superteam's robust attitude to competitiveness and individualism clearly has to be built on a foundation of mutual trust and respect. Superteams don't just get to that point by magic — their members put work into working together, and energy into building key relationships outside the core team; because they recognise that for many people co-operative teamworking doesn't come naturally.

BELIEFS ABOUT PERFORMANCE

Superteam members believe in delivering results. Those results can be looked at in two ways. First there is the technical component of their jobs (the 'what') and here they contribute the benefit of all their specialist education and experience. They are proud of their knowledge, but more they are proud of their ability to apply it to practical problems. And in doing this they bring qualities of creativity and persistence. They see every problem as a challenge. They are optimistic and positive in their approach and are always asking questions like 'How can we do it better?'. Give them a specialist problem and they are as tenacious as terriers until they have it solved.

Unlike many team members we come across, Superteam members do not compromise standards as an easy way out of problems. In one organisation, a company manufacturing, installing and servicing advanced communication equipment, the new product development department allowed a new product to be installed for an important customer before it had been through all the rigorous test procedures. The sales department was pushing hard to be the first into the market before a competitor's product. The inevitable result was a failure of the equipment, a very irate customer and a poor reputation in the market place for reliability. The behaviour of the new product team members in compromising the agreed technical standards, and their failure to confront the issue with sales (breaking another of their team's ground rules) had disastrous results. The happy part of the story is that superb co-operation and teamwork involving members of different departments rescued the situation with the client. Members from new product development, customer service, sales and production worked day and night in shifts to diagnose the problem and manufacture and fit some redesigned components. And all this within seventy-two hours — a fine example of the performance levels the team was capable of.

The second way of looking at members' beliefs about delivering results relates to *how* they work in a team. Superteams develop and articulate their own standards of how they are going to work together when they are 'planning the how'. Their members will work to these standards. The quality that underlies these standards is an intense feeling of responsibility and commitment to others. Superteam members say what they are doing and then do what they say. They are utterly dependable. You can count on them to deliver on time or to give you warning if they can't. They understand how other people are dependent on them and they try to see the situation from those people's point of view. The way that they are seen by others both inside and outside the team is therefore important to them. They want to be seen as reliable, competent and valued team members. They also understand that they are the team's ambassadors to the outside world, and that clients, sponsors, service departments and others are building up their picture of the team and its credibility from their attitudes and actions.

Membership

Suggestions for Superteams

SPOTTING THE GAPS

No team will have amongst its members all the skills and attributes that it requires. But it's as well to be aware of what's missing. A team audit can help which looks at two main areas.

1   Specialist skills and information: team leaders and members should brainstorm the different kinds of experience and expertise that could help them to succeed and then assess what they already have.
2   Teamworking skills and attitudes: Meredith Belbin's book *Management Teams* provides a practical categorisation of different teamworking attributes that a team requires. Members can simply be assessed against these broad categories.

UNBLOCKING YOUR ROLE

In all roles there are *things we must* do and *things we can't* do. These demands and constraints are usually real. But sometimes our view of what we must and cannot do get out of date. The demands and constraints become *imaginary rather than real*.

Team members should therefore check regularly that their assumptions about what they can and can't do, should or shouldn't do are correct. They should also challenge others, particularly when they hear the word 'can't'.

Remember too that 'I can't do X' often really means 'I don't want to do X' or 'I don't know how to do X'. Likewise 'I must do X' often means 'I want to do X'.

CHANGING THE MIX

An international tyre company was concerned about its poor record on product innovation. Amongst other things, a teamworking consultant found that the members of its research and development teams had all been working together for years and were stale. The company decided to move people in and out of teams on a more regular basis. Combined with teambuilding activities, this produced a much improved flow of new ideas and more motivated individuals.

Try moving people in and out of different teams from time to time, especially where a team has been together for a long time.

THE OUTSIDER'S CONTRIBUTION

A different version of 'changing the mix', is to bring outsiders into the team more regularly. More and more teams in organisations are experiencing the benefits of inviting 'outsiders' into the team. They are not so emotionally committed to the team on a day-to-day basis and often bring new perspectives, new contacts and new questions for the team to deal with. Some particularly successful examples are:

- Community representation on local government committees
- Customers involved in new product development teams
- Non-executive directors on company boards
- Sub-contractors more closely involved in their client's team meetings.

Look seriously at how you can bring outsiders into your team, either temporarily or permanently, and what benefit they could bring.

10 The team together

It is only when you are face to face that you're able to see eye to eye.

Jerome Kurtz

Look at the faces of a team when they come out of a meeting and you have a good indication of how it went. Is it smiles and a sense of progress and achievement, or is it a wry look and grumbles about wasted time?

Good meetings don't just happen, they have to be worked at. This chapter looks at some of the strategies and skills that Superteams use to ensure that when they get all the team together, this expensive investment of people's time pays dividends. But first we examine why Superteams attach importance to getting together frequently.

WHY ARE WE COMING TOGETHER?

Some teams have regular meetings which turn into tedious rituals. 'The Monday Morning' meeting can become a joke if it has no real purpose. If a meeting has no real work to do it should be cancelled. Superteams will have some scheduled meetings which act as important milestones. But they are likely to have frequent other meetings, often impromptu or at short notice, and not necessarily involving all the team, but just those who have something they want to talk about together.

Classically, there are three main purposes for meetings:

to communicate information
to solve problems
to make decisions

The skills and strategies that we outline later in this chapter apply to making these kinds of meetings work.

For Superteams, however, these three purposes are only the tip of the iceberg, because under the surface their meetings are fulfilling a number of other important purposes.

Creating identity, cohesion and togetherness

Meetings help to make the team visible. It is the one time when the whole team can be together. Those who are present at the meeting feel they belong to the team. Every member is able to look around and sense the collective identity of which they form a part, and feel the comfort and support which is part of a Superteam.

Producing involvement, ownership and commitment

For each team member, being involved in discussion, contributing ideas and arriving at team decisions produces a feeling of ownership and commitment to those decisions. '*We* came up with that idea and *we* agreed it' said one of our teamworking course participants 'and that means *I* did too. Its *my* idea but its ours too. And that feels good!'

Developing synergy

What do we mean by synergy? The strict definition is producing a whole which is greater than the sum of the parts. It means achieving something as a team that would not be possible for the same individuals to do working singly. Ordinary teams tend to achieve the sum of the efforts of all the members. For Superteams, it is more than that. It is a multiplication rather than an addition, because they spark off each other, and build on each other's ideas and efforts.

Consider for example that Europe, which proportionately has a large number of very brilliant but individualistic scientists, has won relatively few Nobel Prizes, whereas the Massachussets Institute of

Technology, the first research centre to use teams seriously to conduct scientific research, has had seventeen. We can't prove it, but there seems to be a lesson there. 'Close cooperation is better than genius' say the Americans.

Reinforcing the team's ground rules

Superteams develop ground rules designed to help them work well as a team and to produce outstanding individual and team results. Meetings are times when these rules are seen in action, and are reviewed, renewed, or enforced.

Celebrating success

Superteams unashamedly celebrate their successes together. Their celebrations help to generate good morale, and help team members to let go and revitalise after intense periods of work.

They also publicly celebrate individual success by relating stories and giving awards of various kinds. Many companies, and in particular their sales teams, now have regular conferences at which high performers are rewarded and recognised. The events are designed to exchange good news, to enable people to learn from each other, and to associate success with fun and enjoyment.

HOW TO WORK WELL TOGETHER

This is not a book about the skills of running effective meetings. Those are well covered in more specialised books. However, it is a book about what makes Superteams different from ordinary teams.

So, what is it that makes Superteams work better together than ordinary teams? What is it that makes them come out of their meetings tired but exhilarated by a sense of progress, whereas the ordinary team has had a meeting that was 'just routine'. The answer is very simple. Superteams *do* what it says in the books! Ordinary teams talk about it, dabble at it or think that they are doing it, but in practice do not apply the basic disciplines in the systematic, and enthusiastic way of the Superteam.

There is one other important difference too. Because Superteams have worked hard at developing these strategies and skills they can use them almost without thinking. They are unconsciously competent. They use them with the fluid ease and relaxed familiarity of a skilled driver going at speed. The ordinary team however is less experienced, has put less work into achieving fluency and is still at the stage of having to think hard and try hard which makes their performance a bit stilted and self conscious like the learner driver.

We therefore have summarised below what we regard as the *Ten Golden Rules for successfully working together*. They are not comprehensive, but in our experience, if employed regularly soon contribute to improving the team's performance when it is working together.

1. Preparation

The leader should have circulated an agenda and relevant papers sufficiently in advance to allow team members to read and prepare. They in turn will have done some preparatory thinking and will have formulated the main points they want to make. Some prior preparation may well have been done in small sub groups so that the meeting perhaps has to decide between two options put forward by a sub group.

2. Purpose

Leader and members will also have done some thinking about what they want out of the meeting. Often in Superteams, particularly in more spontaneous or informal meetings, all these individual objectives are put on the table at the start of the meeting. The agenda and the purpose or purposes of the meeting then flow from this process. Everyone is quite clear why they are there.

3. Time scheduling

Meetings are often allowed to drift on and either no decisions are taken or decisions rushed through or postponed. Structuring the available time in order to ensure appropriate time is available for each issue will help to achieve the maximum possible in the time you have. Encourage brevity, pithiness and economy of time to help achieve everything that is on the agenda.

4. Creating understanding

There is a range of important interpersonal skills which, if used well, ensure good two-way communication between all members of the team. These are important in all working relationships but especially so when a number of people are working together.

Listening is perhaps the most important skill and discipline which will help a meeting be successful. Listening actively to others by responding to what they have said and then developing their ideas will not only help to achieve the task but will also strengthen relationships within the team.

Asking for clarification in order to clear up confusion, or asking for terms to be defined, are necessary to avoid misunderstandings. This is particularly important if there are different specialists or nationalities in the team.

Summarising helps to keep the group on the right track and checks for understanding. Any team member summarising (and not just the leader) can help to settle one decision or issue before moving on to the next. Similarly summarising is very useful to take stock of progress regularly in mid-discussion.

5. Staying on track

A most common mistake in meetings is for individuals to wander off the subject. This happens in two ways. First the team can be discussing one agenda item and find that the discussion has veered off into another one. Secondly, individual members (and leaders!) introduce hobby horses or red herrings that divert the discussion. It is vital to stick on one issue at a time and finish it off. If the team is to change issues, it should be a conscious and agreed decision. A board of directors for instance was discussing the following year's capital expenditure budget, but decided they could get no further until they had reviewed the latest revenue forecasts which painted a more gloomy picture than the previous set. These latest forecasts clearly had to be discussed before the capital items.

It is equally a waste of time for the team to go over the same ground again and again, like a record stuck in the groove. One team member of such a team commented after a meeting, 'All of this team has a singular ability to flog a dead horse; they talk round and round in circles. Now I know why they have no time to do what they ought to be doing!'

6. Using diverse experience and skills

A good team has a fund of skill and expertise amongst its members which it is foolish to ignore. But using this well means two things.

First the diversity of talent needs to be understood and valued by the team. Equally team members should be open and generous in offering it. Secondly each team member needs to be enabled to participate.

Encouraging active participation of all members of the team especially the quieter ones is an important aspect of the team meetings. How many meetings are there where the leader or one member has dominated the discussion and the rest haven't had a chance to clarify, criticise or give their views. Participation involves most in listening actively while others contribute in turn.

7. The creative problem-solving approach

Think about the old phrase 'He (or she) won't take no for an answer'. Usually it implies that someone is just plain awkward. In an ordinary team this sort of person would probably be seen as a nuisance. Not so in the Superteam. This person would be valued as a problem solver. Problem solvers start from the basic assumption that all problems are solvable. Words like 'can't', 'mustn't', and 'impossible' hardly appear in their vocabulary. Instead they use words like 'what if . . or 'how could we' . . or 'there must be a way to . . .' They are people whose restless minds are always looking for alternatives that might be better. This requires creativity, the ability to invent new solutions for problems linked to the inquisitiveness which is always looking for things that could be improved.

There are, however, many blockages to creativity, especially in teams. Superteams understand about the creative process and are able to use some of the simple techniques which exist to stimulate individual and team creativity. They know also how to use the full diversity of talents in the team as a source of ideas, and how to build and develop other people's ideas. They know too when to leave a problem alone and allow the mind to incubate. And when the moment ·

of illustration comes, the Eureka, they have pencil and paper ready to capture the solution before it disappears.

In ordinary teams people are so busy writing what they hear that they miss most of what is said. Often, too, the best ideas and suggestions in meetings get forgotten. The use of visual aids such as flip charts, which can be stuck around the room, is a valuable tool for recording information and ideas and stimulating thinking.

8. Checking for agreement

'Are we all agreed then?' says the leader, pausing briefly while looking down at the table, 'fine then, we'll go ahead'. This of course cannot be called agreement. Too often the assumption is made by leaders that silence tokens assent. Superteams know that this is a dangerous fantasy. Superteam leaders will always check for assent, particularly in important decisions to which widespread commitment is important. If they forget, their active team members will voice their approval or disapproval without being asked!

CONFLICT

It would be naive to pretend that Superteams are so full of cohesion and commitment that conflict never occurs. Just the opposite. There is probably more conflict in Superteams than in ordinary ones. What is interesting though is the view that Superteams have of that conflict and how they go about resolving it.

Strategies and assumptions

Conflict is a necessary and useful part of team life. Whereas ordinary teams may smooth it over or allow it to become destructive, Superteams look at it directly and do all they can to resolve it to the satisfaction of both parties. Conflict, properly managed and constructively employed, leads to greater understanding amongst the team. Reconciling disagreements, reducing tension, compromising and doing whatever needs to be done for the smooth working of the team is seen as a shared responsibility of each member of the Superteam. Properly managed conflict also provides energy for a team and prevents complacency. Often new ideas emerge out of handling such conflicts which can be used towards the achievement of the team's tasks and objectives.

To produce a constructive and acceptable result, Superteams tend to use two problem-solving approaches in parallel: The first might be summarised as

● *Let us explore ways in which you can achieve what you want without it causing problems for other team members.*

and the second would be

● *Let us explore ways of avoiding or reducing the problems that arise as a result of what you want to do.*

In order to use these problem-solving approaches successfully, the team needs to be able to create an atmosphere in which communication is constructive, open and co-operative. Members employ all their skills to try to understand the different points of view and to find constructive ways out.

Tactics

Sometimes these problem-solving approaches to resolving differences do not or cannot work. In these cases a range of other approaches are used. Here are some that are most frequently used.

● *Sweat it out.* Live through it — it will eventually be over.

● *Wear them down.* Keep pushing until they have no more energy to continue the conflict.

● *Appeal to higher principles.* Rise above individual conflict and focus on 'what's good for the team as a whole'.

● *Drop it.* Does it really matter that much? Why not give in? Don't isolate people — it's more important to keep the team together.

● *Send a diplomat.* Send an emissary from the team to smooth the way before the team gets together.

● *Distancing.* Separate out the tasks of the people involved in the conflict. Make them less interdependent.

• *Negotiate*. Negotiate within the group. Be prepared to bargain and compromise.

• *Third-party*. Consult a third party who will act as an honest broker between the parties in conflict. Perhaps a sponsor or someone outside the team.

• *Try coercion*. If all else fails, invoke the authority of the leader to decide who wins.

IS THERE LIFE AFTER MEETINGS?

If you've just read our Ten Golden Rules for working well together, you may have noticed that we deliberately left two out. We did this first because we think they are so important that they merit headings of their own and second because we think it is fitting to finish off this chapter with two of the most important constituents of the 'Hallmark of Superteams'.

9. Review the working of the team

Superteams are self critical. They are never satisfied with their own performance. And so at the end of meetings they will spend some time talking about how it went. Feedback will be brief but honest and ideas will be put forward for improvement. At the same time the team may conduct a broader review of how they are working. This is the time when they examine the ground rules they have developed in Planning the How to make sure they are still appropriate and working well.

10. Action

After all the talking and discussion, the Superteam will swing into action. For *action* is above all the 'Hallmark of the Superteam'.

Recognising the threats to action that come when the individual team members disperse, the leader will ensure that all actions are summarised and agreed at the end of the meeting. Furthermore the individuals responsible will be identified and the deadline for completion will be specified. This summary will be circulated to all concerned certainly within twenty-four hours to act as a reminder. Too often these sorts of details appear in the minutes which come the day before the *next* meeting — the time by which many of the actions probably should have been completed.

In between meetings, the leader will be making contact with members to monitor progress and help accomplishment of the agreed actions in any way possible.

The Team Together

Suggestions for Superteams

THE MEETING ROOM

- Get comfortable upright chairs and a large enough table for people to spread their papers.
- Try a square, round or oval table rather than a long thin rectangular one.
- Have two flip chart stands and space all round the walls to hang flip charts on if necessary.
- Ensure no disturbances during the meeting.

MAINTAINING ENERGY

- Make sure the room is well ventilated and not too hot.
- Take short 'mind-breaks' at regular intervals. People don't concentrate fully for more than about an hour. A five-minute break buys another hour's concentration.
- Use creativity techniques such as brainstorming if the ideas are drying up and the meeting gets a bit flat.
- Change the 'norm' that people should sit down during meetings. Stand up and walk around. It's stimulating.
- Have cold drinks easily available.

BRINGING THE OUTSIDE IN

- Invite important members of your invisible team to attend your meetings either as observers or as participants if a subject concerning them is on the agenda.

115

- Invite outsiders in when the team is trying to think of alternatives/improved ways of doing things. They can often see ways that you can't.

TEAM IDENTITY

- Have a special room put aside which is clearly identified as the team's territory.
- Devise a name and a logo for the team. Use it frequently to others. Put it on letters, sweatshirts, doors of team member's offices and anywhere else visible.

KEEP IT SNAPPY

- Hold frequent short meetings rather than infrequent long ones.
- Set a time limit for the meeting and allocate time to each agenda item accordingly.
- Appoint someone as time-keeper.

TRY T–A–T (Together–Apart–Together)

- Don't always get stuck in the notion that the team has to stay together throughout a meeting. So for instance:

    Make it OK for people to leave the meeting for a period if the agenda item is of no interest to them.

    Deliberately split the meeting into sub groups for a period. This can be especially valuable if a team is grappling with a multifaceted problem. Each sub group can look at a different aspect and then report back. This technique saves time, stops the meeting getting bogged down, re-energises people and often makes quicker progress than the whole team could together.

SILLY TIME

Leaders of teams should be aware that when members of a team have been apart for a long time they need to get to know each other again and re-form the team. You should allow some informal unstructured time for this bonding process to go on. We call it silly time because it is often spent catching up on gossip and light-hearted banter — anything but work! But it is important.

An alternative to silly time is all to meet socially the night before the formal meeting fixed for the next morning.

USE THE TEN GOLDEN RULES

Have them printed on a large sheet of paper and hung up on the wall in your meeting room. Spend time at the end of the meeting reviewing how well the team and each member applied them and agree what you're going to work on doing better next time. Then DO IT!

11 The team apart

Things fall apart, the centre cannot hold

Yeats

(When the team is dispersed) other team members, although out of sight, should not be out of mind.

Colin Hill, Shell UK

The conventional image of a team is a number of people working together in a room or having a meeting round a table. Approaches to developing teams have dealt almost exclusively with this aspect of a team's working.

Yet, experience and observation in organisations repeatedly suggest that things start to go wrong, or get worse when the meeting is over, when the team disperses, and goes away 'to get on with the real work'. It is also true to say that the lion's share of a team's 'work' is done by individuals allocated certain tasks for completion between formal meetings. It's true also, that much of the contact between team members happens informally when the team is apart.

The critical skill that members of Superteams develop for working apart is the ability to imagine the impact that their actions and decisions are having on others. They have to be self-disciplined enough (and care enough) to ask colleagues for information and to keep them informed of their own progress. These problems of communication and co-ordination have to be resolved against a stressful backdrop. One manager, who had undertaken to do an assignment for the general management team of which she was a member, found great difficulty fitting it in around her other responsibilities. Her commitments as leader of her own team and the daily demands of her customers at a particularly busy time of year proved too heavy. She signalled the problem to her colleagues and they found a way to share out the burden. The leader of a temporary project team was also a member of two others, and in addition was struggling to hold down a regular line-job. Pressures on team members produce conflicts of priority which come to the fore when the team is apart. Physical separation of plants and offices, and language and cultural differences can also cause misunderstandings which can exacerbate the problems of the team apart.

It is when the team is apart that its resources are most stretched. That is when it is most vulnerable, and when it is most difficult for the leader to monitor progress or to hold it all together. Putting all the responsibility onto the leader for co-ordination invariably leads to disastrous results. It is simply too much to handle. Superteams therefore share the responsibility for keeping the team on track by developing ground rules for working apart.

For individualistic team members the implementation of these ground rules will not come easily and ways of reminding and helping may be needed. The leader must again both monitor and motivate without being stifling and interfering. The team must find ways to check progress regularly, and particularly amongst those individuals whose tasks are interdependent. Areas of interdependence must be clearly mapped out so that members understand about how other people in the team are affected by their work.

GREAT EXPECTATIONS

Who does what and when

The leaders and members of Superteams have high expectations of each other when working apart. Before the team splits up to work apart, they will have a clear idea of what each person is mandated to do. Each team member acts with delegated authority. Team members see that their roles are central to others, and develop a greater sense of responsibility to do what they have said they will do. Each person is seen as a team ambassador and is entrusted with the responsibility to manage those outside the team that they come into contact with.

Deciding and agreeing what is expected of the team when it is apart is therefore essential. How often in ordinary teams does one hear the comment 'The right hand doesn't know what the left hand is doing'. Superteams ensure that this does not happen. The confusion about the right hand not knowing what the left hand is doing creates conflicts among the team members, and makes the team look incompetent to outsiders. It also frequently leads to either duplication or wasting of effort.

One of our clients in the publishing world commented: 'Every time our meetings break up, I have a sense that the team is really breaking apart. Even when decisions are made, I'm never confident that they will be implemented. We are terrible at follow up and follow through'.

In Superteams each person undertakes publicly to take certain actions and achieve certain results within specified periods of time. Everyone understands what the rules are when the team breaks up to work apart.

HOLDING ON AND LETTING GO

When the team is apart it needs to be able to hold on and to let go simultaneously. It holds on to the team's values, expectations and standards, but it lets go of the comfort and cohesiveness of being *with* the other members of the team. For team members too, they have to hold on to their priorities and let go of the distractions that divert their energy.

Autonomy and responsibility

To a large extent when the Superteam is apart, the responsibility is thrown on to the team's members to be the guardians of the team's objectives, expectations, standards and values.

They have to be able to let go of the security that comes from being together. It is a time to stand alone, and to exercise the autonomy that many of them cherish. Now each individual *is* the team or at least the team's representative when apart. When the team is apart, each member is promoting the reputation of the team, and publicising its work, while at the same time continuing to do what needs to be done in order to deliver excellent results. The team member needs to hold on to the lines of support provided by the leader but let go of the apron strings and work responsibly alone. It is at such times that independent individuals can often make their best contribution provided they conform to the ground rules laid down by the team.

The leader in turn needs to let go of individual team members. Superteam leaders are able to trust the members to meet deadlines, trust their commitment and dedication and let go of the tasks that have been delegated to them. Interference through distrust or anxiety will only produce a negative reaction.

Distractions

Events occurring outside require responses by team members. They often require members to make sacrifices of time and effort. So members individually have to be able to handle themselves in these circumstances, and remain focused on their priorities. For example, one public sector team leader commented:

> Events in the outside world affect us and make life difficult. Our team members are vulnerable to this influence. Sometimes continuous demands from the public, though legitimate, distract and undermine what the team is really trying to do. It puts immense pressure on our team members, especially when they may have to work alone over long periods of time.

Being able to set priorities, use time effectively, and reduce unwanted distractions are all immensely valuable skills for team leaders and members in these circumstances. If certain members of Superteams are under particular pressure that they cannot control, then they ask for help. Often the leader can act as a shield for them by handling some of the pressure. At other times colleagues may help or the time scales for completion are renegotiated within the team.

MAINTAINING MOMENTUM AND COMMITMENT

It is far easier to create excitement over a compelling vision at the start of a project or when the team is all together then to keep it in mind when working apart. In the case of Superteams, sustaining enthusiasm and commitment over a long period of time is a matter of both the personal persistence and motivation of team members and the strength and amount of support they have from the leader and the rest of the team.

The part-time team

The biggest problem for team members is the tendency for day-to-day routine activities to take precedence over the actions agreed by the team. Particularly where team members have a number of other responsibilities, it is most important for the leader to provide a constant reminder of priorities. This can be done in a positive way by communicating the helicopter view and continuing to remind the team members of the vision towards which they are working. Without interfering with the working of team members the leader must try and keep them motivated. One way is to use the support of the sponsor from time to time. The leader might arrange for a well-timed visit or a letter congratulating the team on progress so far reminding everyone how important the team work is to the organisation. The leader needs to keep in touch with each member, to be available when needed and to provide support. In this way the leader can ensure that each member keeps on track, maintains momentum and commitment and delivers the results which were agreed in advance.

There will be times, however, when the pressure on the part-time team leader or member will be too great, and slippage will start to occur. At this stage the leader will need to renegotiate the 'contract' with the sponsor or try to do some sort of deal with those who control the other aspects of the team member's responsibilities. In one instance a woman in a large retail store was involved in two task forces as well as doing a line personnel job. The task was proving impossible. The leaders and sponsors of the two task forces met together with the personnel manager. They concluded that her role in one of the task forces was vital to the company and that only she could do it. She was also particularly enjoying the developmental opportunity afforded by the other one. After considerable discussion of alternatives, the personnel manager agreed that she could hand over half of her line responsibilities to other members of the personnel department for a fixed period of three months only while the task force work was completed.

The full-time team

Even if the team members are working full time in the team, maintaining momentum is equally important. One particularly good leader of a production team, split across different sites and different shifts, ensured that he held regular meetings, put out weekly progress reports and was seen often walking the shop floor. He was also easily contactable to help solve problems. This team leader was superb at demonstrating the value of each individual's contribution to the team and constantly reminded them of how their part fitted into the big picture. He also made his team members highly aware of their responsibilities to each other. Arising from this the team developed a common and agreed procedure and checklist for handing over between two shifts — a classic case of the team apart where problems occur. The result was a dramatic reduction in problems and misunderstandings between shifts.

ACTIVE COMMUNICATIONS

Communications are relatively easy when the team is together. Misunderstandings can be ironed out, clarification sought, and ideas exchanged and built on. When the team is apart, communications become more difficult and yet it is at this stage that the team most needs to keep in touch. The team leader and members have to take *active* steps to communicate.

Superteams of course use all the normal methods of communication when working apart. But they also recognise the importance of informal communications. Often, for instance those people working in close physical proximity will get together for a quick impromptu meeting, or just to spend time with each other. Lunch dates, chatting in corridors, frequent telephone calls, and meeting socially outside work are particularly important. The team members make their own informal links, not always relying on the leader to be the person asking for and exchanging information.

Staying in touch

Superteams share the responsibility for maintaining communications. Although the leader's role is central, team members take responsibility not only to communicate how they are doing but to check and monitor how the rest of the team is doing. One leader of a Sales and Marketing team commented: 'The most productive use of my time when the team is dispersed is "communication" — it's very important to give them information and that when they ask for information they receive it quickly. It's not typically done in this organisation and it is time consuming. But, it does have real benefits. It keeps ownership and commitment alive. It keeps everybody focused on the importance of the job, and it makes them feel that they still belong'.

In our own team, we do not always find it easy to keep each other informed, especially when we are working in different locations or working abroad. Having discussed the issue, we decided to invest in a system of telephone answering machines at our homes as well as at our office where our administrative coordinator acts as a link. We can listen in to these machines from anywhere in the world. This has helped us to maintain contact and remain in touch with each other.

The leader's role when the team is apart is rather like a spider weaving a web. She's at the centre but constantly making the links between one point and another. Staying in touch with individuals and passing information between different members and from the centre to the members is the heart of the leader's contribution to the team apart.

Signalling problems early

Active communications are particularly important when there are problems. In ordinary teams, problems often make team members withdraw. They struggle to solve them by themselves and in so doing lose contact with the team.

Superteams, however, have a ground rule that any problems, particularly if they may affect others, are signalled early. As the climate in Superteams is one of problem solving, there is little need to hide problems. Sharing problems, asking for help and saying you're stuck is part of the way they do things. Blame is not assigned to the person with the problem. The question asked is how do we overcome it?

Serious failures, the ones that leave deep scars on teams, are usually ones where the signs of the problem have been there but no one has picked them up or they've been ignored. Such situations rarely occur in Superteams. The exchange of information is frequent, fast and frank. Team members don't ignore or hide the bad news. They recognise how easy it is to do this when they are working apart, but they also recognise the devastating effect it can have on the team's progress and cohesiveness. For the one cardinal sin of Superteam members is to let a fellow team member down.

The Team Apart
Suggestions for Superteams

MODERN TECHNOLOGY

- Use modern information technology to help the team to communicate when apart — for instance

  Computer networks linking members of the team in different offices and sites.
  Telephone or television conferences.
  Telephone answering machines.
  Radio paging systems.
  Car telephones.

INFORMAL COMMUNICATION

- Have a team notice board which team members pass regularly preferably near a communal meeting place such as a coffee machine. Pin up the team's main objectives as well as the short term priorities. Also have a section where members can leave messages for each other, and ask for ideas from team members or outsiders.

- Have a good secretary, co-ordinator or personal assistant for the leader who can act as an information puller and pusher at the centre. This person should always be asking 'who needs to know what and when'.

- Fix with fellow team members who work nearby that you will meet once a week over lunch for a gripe and groan session (otherwise known in Superteams as a hype and help session).

- Talk to each other regularly on the telephone. If you haven't heard from some of them for a while, give them a ring and show interest in what they're doing.

DOING THE ROUNDS

- If the team is geographically dispersed, rotate meetings round the different sites on a regular basis. Give the local team member the responsibility for organising the meeting room and all administrative and social arrangements. Also build in a special presentation or tour by local team members describing in detail their part of the team's work.
- Team leaders should practise MBWA (Management by Walking About). Visit your team members regularly, especially those at remote locations.

FORMAL COMMUNICATION

- Schedule team together meetings at regular intervals to provide milestones and to reinforce team identity.

- Publish deadlines, agreed action plans and responsibilities immediately after meetings.

- Ask for brief but regular written progress reports from members that get circulated round the whole team. A standard, punchy format helps.

- Publish a regular report or news sheet showing progress made, successes achieved, future forecasts and problems anticipated.

PART THREE
Teamworking Projects

PUTTING TEAMWORK INTO PRACTICE

The case histories described in the next seven chapters illustrate the range of practical teamworking strategies projects that many organisations are now pursuing. There is no simple approach that is best — that will depend on the needs, opportunities and practical constraints in each different situation.

Chapter 12 is the story of how Buttermouth, a public agency involved teams in the development and implementation of a new strategy.

Chapter 13 relates the teamworking approach used by NCMT, an engineering company, to ensure the success of a restructuring exercise.

Chapter 14 describes how team development activities contributed to the successful merger of National Bank and Commercial Investment Services.

Chapter 15 is a short case study of a project team within an organisation — in this case co-ordinating the installation of a new telephone system at Radbridge University.

Chapter 16 shows how Logicorp, an electronics company, went about preserving good teamworking between different departments at a time of rapid growth.

Chapter 17 describes what was involved after the main board of Springkleen, a household products manufacturer, decided they wanted to fine tune their teamworking.

Chapter 18 outlines how RDL International, a research and development organisation, went about developing a pool of competent team leaders to manage projects.

12 Strategy development and implementation

Buttermouth is a small but highly visible public agency charged with the conservation of an area of outstanding natural beauty, providing facilities for visitors and helping to maintain the local community.

The government body responsible for Buttermouth had commissioned a report to look at how to improve economy, efficiency and effectiveness of this and other public agencies. As a result of this audit and various issues identified through the newly implemented appraisal system, Buttermouth had recognised a number of areas for development and improvement.

THE PROBLEM

How to organise and prepare Buttermouth to meet the challenges of the future and become even more successful than it currently was

For its size, Buttermouth had a very high diversity and complexity of functions and had achieved very real and consistent successes. It had also attracted a very high calibre of people to work for it, who between them brought an enviable level and range of practical and professional skills. These people were held together by a unique, shared vision — love of and commitment to preserving their natural environment.

The will to develop Buttermouth was clearly present in the senior management team and at other levels in the organisation. However, there was anxiety about the demands that the future would place on people who worked there, Buttermouth, and how the organisation could respond.

Initial discussions highlighted three broad issues facing the organisation.

- **Shared vision, direction and strategy**

Although there was a tremendous amount of individual commitment, it needed to be harnessed. A 'common' objective was missing. The immediate task for the top team was to develop a strategy for the development of the organisation. Furthermore, individuals needed an increased sense of involvement in setting Buttermouth's objectives through increased participation, involvement and communication.

- **Organisational structures**

Buttermouth was not sure that they had the right organisational structure to deliver the improved results required. They wanted to utilise current resources better, target individual performance better, and to evolve a structure towards smaller mixed teams, with greater responsibility and accountability. To do this they realised the need for better management information systems and managerial skills.

- **Internal/external communications**

Buttermouth's image externally was confused. They also felt that there was considerable scope for mobilising public opinion better. In addition, with employees on remote sites, the need for better internal information was recognised.

THE APPROACH

Buttermouth called in teamworking consultants to help them to change the organisation from a 'do your own thing culture' to a 'teamworking culture'. At the same time they wanted to evolve a strategy for the future of the organisation.

Interviews on future strategy

The consultants interviewed all twenty-one senior officers of Buttermouth who had been identified as a core group to be involved in strategy development and implementation. Their views were sought on future directions for the organisation and the capabilities needed to get there. They were also asked to identify the current strengths of the organisation and any problem areas.

Report

After the analysis of the interview data, the consultants prepared a report outlining major strategic issues to be resolved, and putting forward some tentative recommendations on how this might be achieved. The report was circulated to all twenty-one interviewees and feedback indicated broad agreement with the analysis.

Training

One recommendation was the formation of five strategy groups, each to look at a different aspect of Buttermouth's activities. The idea was that membership would cut across the current rather rigid departmental boundaries to start encouraging greater teamwork and a wider perspective in strategy development.

As the group of twenty-one officers were not very familiar with working in teams the consultants held a one-day training programme to introduce basic teamworking skills. The group also discussed how best the strategy groups could be helped to work well.

Strategy groups — Planning the What

Five cross-departmental strategy groups were set up. These groups covered external relations, managing visitors, managing the landscape, the local economy and management information systems. Each strategy group was assigned a 'sponsor' from the senior management team. Sponsors were to act as a link between the strategy group and the senior management team. Each strategy group also had an appointed leader.

The strategy groups had a broad brief from the senior management team to review current strategy in their designated area. They were also asked to suggest innovative alternatives for the future and to recommend any changes that the senior management team could consider for inclusion in the Buttermouth development strategy. Each group's report was circulated to everyone.

Strategy groups — Planning the How

Other reasons for setting up the strategy groups included:

- to encourage teamworking and the involvement of staff at all levels in the Buttermouth development strategy, in order fully to utilise the organisation's resources of knowledge and skills.
- to create a view that Buttermouth was likely to become a dynamic rather than static organisation, subject to more constant change.
- to secure greater commitment to the implementation of each group's recommendations once approved by the Senior Management team.
- to develop in individual team members a wider and deeper understanding of the range and complexity of Buttermouth's activities, and some of the constraints within which it operated.

Presentation of group findings

A one-day meeting was held, where each strategy group presented their findings to the total group, the senior management team and the consultants. After the presentations and questions of clarification, the senior management team responded to the recommendations put forward indicating those areas that they were prepared to sponsor in the short and long term, and also indicating some issues on which they thought more work needed doing before a final decision.

Further opportunities were provided for individuals to give the senior management team and the consultants their private views on the implications of the recommendations, particularly as regards a restructuring of the organisation to support the emerging new strategy.

The senior management team, together with the consultants, spent time formulating the development strategy for Buttermouth and a tentative implementation plan including options on restructuring. These were discussed at another full group meeting and after some modification were agreed with all parties for recommendation to the Board, elected and appointed officials overseeing Buttermouth's activities.

COMMENTARY

The approach taken at Buttermouth is a good example of one kind of team-based approach to strategy development and implementation. The first purpose of this kind of approach is to develop better strategy by utilising the wider resources of the organisation outside the top team. The second purpose is to gain greater commitment to it by making those who will implement it stakeholders in its development.

The approach is both 'top down' and 'bottom up'. The senior management team used their authority to give a lead and set broad directions and parameters for the groups. The strategy groups in turn provided new ideas to a senior team that was willing to listen and accept but also not afraid to reject and explain why. On many occasions too there was argument and persuasion as each side won the other round to its point of view. Through this interactive process the strategy and priorities emerged, its implementation being directly considered and evaluated in the process. Through this interaction too the role, power, authority and credibility of both sides were enhanced as they struggled with common problems.

Besides its stated purpose of strategy development, however, this teamworking approach was also having complex effects of perhaps even greater importance for the organisation. First, it was breaking down existing barriers between departments as people who had never really come together before worked on issues. Second, it provided a new teamworking model for the organisation as people saw the benefits of co-operation between specialists. Multidisciplinary teams were in fact recommended subsequently for a revised structure — a radical departure from previous practice. Thirdly, all the individuals involved, from the senior management team downwards, developed significantly as new demands were placed on them and as they broadened and deepened their understanding of their own organisation. And, finally, the process led to a much quicker and more complete understanding amongst the implementers of precisely what they were trying to achieve, and a greater confidence and conviction in securing the commitment of others at the implementation stages.

It is teamworking strategies and approaches such as these that are revolutionising the way that organisations develop their strategies. No longer need strategy be seen as the product of a senior team divorced from reality. No longer need strategy be a set of good intentions expressed in a corporate plan but which fail to change the way the organisation goes about its business.

13 Restructuring

NCMT is a large engineering group that has committed itself to shifting its production from production line principles toward a team-based working system. The largest site is responsible for the production and final assembly of sophisticated, numerically controlled machine tools. Some components are manufactured at other sites and transferred for assembly.

The concept of a team-based system was initiated at top management level, although it was handed over to local site management for implementation. Site management was aware of precedents set by other parts of the group but was convinced that there was considerable advantage to be had from developing an independent system specifically geared to meeting local conditions.

Immediately prior to our first contact two important decisions had been made. A keen and articulate advocate of the team-based system had been transferred from another site to take operational control of the new system as team co-ordinator. This new role in effect superceded the role of site manager. Secondly, a group of eight had been recruited from the existing production organisation to become leaders of eight proposed new teams.

It is also important to be aware that the organisation had decided on a programme of investment in building alterations. The intention was to give each team its own physical location to serve as office, meeting point and nerve centre for team operations.

THE PROBLEM

How to develop a team-based production organisation which would lead to improvements in product quality, costs and delivery

Some of the important issues were communicated to us by the client and others fell out of early discussions with a wide range of people affected by the change. They can be summarised as follows.

Team design

● Who should be included as members of the core teams? The production function was supported by a number of support services such as production planning, maintenance and management services. To what extent should staff from these service functions become fully integrated members of the new production teams bearing in mind the resources and the inconsistency of demand from the teams.

Developing commitment to the change

The team co-ordinator put it succinctly — 'What I want is teams committed to doing a good job and capable of managing their own day-to-day affairs, solving their own problems and not coming to me for approval of every action or decision they take'.

● How to convince team-members and especially the new team-leaders that the new system is worth going for and that senior management is sincere in its desire to make the team organisation work, and to provide the necessary training and development support.

Planning for lift-off

● Who should be responsible for planning the transition and at what stage should team leaders and other key team members be brought into the picture?

● How much detailed planning should be done up-front and how far could early experience of the new structure be used to complement and feed the planning process?

Developing team leaders

Having been recruited from senior supervisory positions, most of the team leaders were new to the responsibilities of management and especially to managing teams.

• What could be done to increase their self-confidence and develop appropriate new skills, attitudes and behaviour to meet the exacting demands of the new role?

The problem of the team leaders' development was compounded by long-established supervisory habits which inhibited their effectiveness as team-leaders.

• How to get them to stand back, reflect how their teams were working, diagnose and cure problems, delegate, make decisions and maintain a clear vision of the purpose and objectives of the new team structure.

Developing team members

Although the developmental needs of those in other managerial roles within the teams were similar in many respects to those of team leaders, there were some other requirements. They had not been so extensively involved in early discussions during which the change was consolidated.

• How to raise their awareness of the nature and implications of the change for their own roles?

• What would be the key differences between the supervisory role in the existing organisation and their new managerial role in the team-based system?

THE APPROACH

We were concerned that the emphasis on change should not extinguish the value of existing strengths. This was particularly important in dealing with team leaders and their first level managers. Some of their anxiety came from an assumption that the introduction of the new system would undermine their existing competence.

In arriving at the form of our help to the client we were aware of some important considerations.

- The change was to become effective within a month of our first contact with the client. We had to respond quickly to identify the priorities.
- The need to create self-sufficient teams quickly, in order to get the new system operational.
- The need to build-up a co-operative and open dialogue between senior personnel and team leaders in preparation for going live.
- The great importance of developing mechanisms to support the teams and team leaders in the first few months, a period which would inevitably bring some failures, many doubts and considerable uncertainty.
- The likelihood that senior management might demand clear evidence of success too early on. The fear was that their impatience might prejudice success or that they may revert to the known and the familiar, whatever its weaknesses.

The first workshop

This included all eight team leaders and three functional heads of the main support services. The workshop took place over a period of five days. It was to be the launching pad from which the new system would take off and it was planned that the new system would go into operation immediately following the workshop.

Senior management saw the workshop as a crucial opportunity to signal the importance of the change, to reaffirm the value it attached to the role of the team leaders, and the support it was prepared to give. The focus of the workshop was on the strategic purpose and operational demands of the new system and included:

- Creating a shared vision of the new team-based system and gaining commitment to it.

- Identifying areas of significant change in operational requirements from the current system.

- Developing a new 'blueprint' to serve as a set of principles and groundrules for all new teams.

- Negotiating a set of acceptable success criteria with senior management (both short and medium term).

- Presentation of the vision and blueprint to senior management followed by detailed discussion to reach agreement on the resourcing implications and to clarify other features of the blueprint, raised by either side.

- Agreeing with senior management a new set of expectations regarding responsibility and authority, where it was located, where it came from and how it was to be used. The notion of decentralised teams managing their own destinies required as much change in senior management attitudes as in team leaders' attitudes.

- Re-negotiating the relationship with senior representatives from support services, to ensure that teams would receive the right responses. This included establishing more open communication between teams and support services, an agreement to avoid 'unreasonable demands', allaying support service concerns about loss of authority and 'being taken over', and agreeing procedures for handling conflicts of interest.

- Establishing a mutual support team among team-leaders as a 'safe-house' which would provide a forum for accelerating their development by regular discussion and exchange of experience, as well as a mechanism for identifying and solving issues common to all the teams.

- Introduce team leaders and support service managers to the Ashridge Team-Working Approach as a way of describing simply what was happening and as a basis for diagnosing areas for further team development.

- Identify strategies for team leaders to begin the process of building their own teams and developing their first line managers.

The second workshop series

These were designed for the development of first line managers within the new teams. Each lasted three days and the series took place over a one year period following the introduction of the new system. The aims of each workshop were:

- To check out the first line managers' understanding of the new system and identify key operational issues.

- Improve skills in managing relationships with each other and with the team leader as well as managing the performance of their people.

- Introduce them to the Ashridge Team-Working Approach and give experience of working in a high performance team during the workshop.

- Identify the key demands of their role in supporting the team leader, and in liaising with support services.

- Negotiate with team leaders and clarify the success criteria of their role.

- Develop a network of contacts across the different teams to exchange learning and to prevent teams becoming insular.

Return of the team leaders

We met team leaders formally again about six months into the new system. For three days, attention was given to the following:

- Re-affirming the vision and focusing on successes in order to check out that the direction was still right, that commitment was still there and that the real purposes were being achieved.

- Identify problems which had been experienced and work through options to resolve them.

- With the priority which had to be given to operational issues during the first workshop, more attention was given here to making the Ashridge Team-Working Approach more explicit through the use of exercises to demonstrate aspects of the approach particularly relevant to the team leader's role.

- Meetings at the request of senior management to hear how they might improve their sponsorship of the new system.

Ongoing

In between all the formal events described above, we were in regular contact with all parties concerning acting as catalysts, monitors, reminders and problem solvers.

COMMENTARY

Restructuring is frequently a messy business. In this case the decision was made to invest heavily to ensure that the new organisation was able to start operating effectively in the shortest possible time, and that this was subsequently sustained.

The NCMT situation highlights two fundamental issues that need to be confronted in most restructuring. The first is that changes of structure (and strategy too) do not merely create new groupings and reporting relationships but usually demand new skills and attitudes from those concerned. Secondly, changes such as these create enormous uncertainty and anxiety. The workshops we describe here were therefore fulfilling important functions both in training and development terms and also in reducing uncertainty.

Uncertainty is reduced in a number of ways. Bringing groups together to be briefed on the purpose of the new structure is a simple first step. Allowing those groups then to work out how to make it work, giving them the power to plan their own destinies, reduces the negative consequences of uncertainty hugely by enabling people to feel in control. Bringing key members of the invisible team, the service departments, into the team was also a significant step in reducing the unknown. Making them develop the new groundrules for their working relationship then put the final piece in the jigsaw.

Too frequently, restructuring causes both confusion and inefficiency with little or no clear benefits in the long term. Well handled, recognising that restructuring creates new teams that require new groundrules if they are to operate successfully, restructuring is a potent way of redirecting energy within an organisation. Investment in managing the uncertainty and providing the necessary training for these new teams can have significant payoffs in ensuring that new structures are quickly implanted and that the planned benefits materialise in practice.

14 Joint ventures and mergers

National Bank (NB) and Commercial Investment Services (CIS) were two autonomous businesses within a large financial group. A secret consultant's report recommended a merger of the two companies including bringing together two independent head offices. The purpose of the proposed merger was to gain strength in providing clients with a more comprehensive range of financial services. Each had for some time been encroaching on the other's activities and the distinction between the two has become increasingly blurred and difficult to justify.

The Main Board of the group, having accepted the consultant's proposals, set up a small corporate task force of three Board Members which was given a period of four months to establish how the change could be made to happen so that existing service levels would still be guaranteed while at the same time demonstrating the advantage both to the customers and to the two constituent companies.

The new organisation, Natcom Services, was to become the group's 'flag-ship' and serve as a test bed for developing a new responsiveness to growing opportunities in the financial services markets. It was also to bolster the group's ability to compete, especially with rapidly growing, highly competent and professionally dedicated competition from the US.

The cultures of the two businesses were visibly in conflict. National

Bank was prestigious, conservative, arrogant and very introspective with a heavy bias towards administrative systems. Commercial Investment Services on the other hand was pragmatic, outgoing, sales-oriented and dynamic. Each viewed the other with some suspicion.

THE PROBLEM

How to bring these two distinctive cultures together in a collaborative merger which would capitalise on the strengths of both, stimulate synergy, and improve performance through a broader professional base, entrepreneurship and new products and services

Specific issues needed to be faced if the merger was going to succeed. They had to be dealt with quickly and positively. The corporate task force expressed them as follows:

Thinking big

The new venture could readily be sabotaged by either company, especially by powerful and influential senior personnel. One thing each had in common was a strong sense of being right. Each firm believed that growth and success would be best promoted by doing more of what it was good at. Implicit was the belief that the 'other needs to be like us'.

● How to bring the two together in such a way that both would be encouraged to reformulate a large new vision towards which both could contribute while at the same time, preserving what was good about each. Developing a joint strategy for the new business, was an urgent need.

Ownership

The suspicion that each would push hard to have the merger on its own terms was inescapable. The Main Board was committed to appointing the current General Manager of CIS as Chief Executive of Natcom Services. An outstanding innovator, he was young (late thirties) driving and had a proven track record for building a good team. Several other CIS staff were tipped for key positions in the merged business.

The General Manager of NB had accepted early retirement but this was kept very quiet and he was not due to go until a year into the life of the new operation. A straight, respected autocrat, he dispensed approval to the loyal, of which there were many. He had been told confidentially about the proposed merger and had reacted adversely, stating his intention of refusing to co-operate and not taking any part in communicating the change to his staff as long as he was there.

• How to 'sell' the new Chief Executive without fuelling speculation of a takeover of NB by CIS. If rumours of this kind were to gain currency, NB staff might be expected to lose face and more important, become unco-operative. It was vital to the merger to be able to avoid any suggestion that its primary purpose was to strengthen a weak business in NB. Each business had unique but qualitatively different strengths to trade in.

Communicating the merger

The corporate task force was convinced that announcing the merger from the centre would only promote speculation and rumour. Statements would ideally be made by local management at a time when substantial and credible information could be made available. The favoured mechanism was one where the new top-team Natcom Services appeared together.

• How to bring members of the new Natcom Services top team together to agree an approach to communicating the merger unambiguously to the separate businesses, and to ensure that the message was the same for each.

Fast or slow

Should the merger be served through a fast-moving coup or through a process of controlled evolution taking perhaps several months to complete? Each had certain important advantages. Moving fast would create initial shock, but offer an opportunity for rapid recovery based on the need to manage the new organisation. The disadvantage would be the need to plan in detail in advance.

Moving more leisurely would be less disruptive in an environment where business had to continue, could start sooner and could use early small-scale experiments as a source of experience for developing more sophisticated plans. It would mean though that the change process would continue over a much longer period.

• How to confirm one of these options recognising that the new Natcom top team would be responsible for its implementation.

Extending the team

Mergers do not lend themselves readily to advanced publicity. Inevitably the new top team at Natcom would be at the centre of decision-making. The task force recognised, however, the considerable payoffs to be had from extending the net to include a larger group of people from the two businesses who would be in the forefront of efforts to develop co-operation. At a later stage it would be necessary to gain the commitment of others at an operational level who would be vital to raising the overall performance standards of the new organisation.

Dealing with rumours

At the time of the proposed merger, uncertainty had been generated by frequent and significant changes in senior management in both NB and CIS. The effect was to create waves of speculation and rumour. Much of it assumed that some draconian change was imminent including ironically, the possibility that CIS was going to be divested. In fact this movement of senior personnel was independent of the merger and was a feature of an ongoing process of moving successful, younger people into areas of significant responsibility to counter the growing threat from an ageing senior management population.

THE APPROACH

Working with the corporate task force

By the time we were invited in, news of the existence of the corporate task force had leaked out to senior management in both NB and CIS. We had met the latter in an informal setting briefly. From them we learned that there was great suspicion at the secretive and apparently conspiratorial way that the corporate task group was working. If the idea was to keep a low profile on the merger, the silence was deafening.

As soon as we met the corporate task force it became apparent that they were experiencing difficulty and were floundering in something of a vacuum. They had no first hand information to work on. After getting them to explore a number of options for moving forward, they decided, with the Board's sanction, to appoint the five members of the new Natcom Services senior management team, (two from NB and three from CIS) and to invite them into their task force. This extended group became known as the steering group, and they asked us to continue to work with them.

Working with the steering group

The steering group presented a number of opportunities to begin the process of working out how the merger could be skilfully implemented to ensure that it achieved its business objectives.

First it presented an ideal opportunity to begin to work out a common vision for the merger and start work on the provisional Big Picture outlining the main steps in implementing the merger.

Secondly it presented an opportunity to develop trust between some senior managers of NB and CIS to secure their confidence, and to begin to build the new top team, together with their corporate sponsors.

Having helped them to allocate their priorities, they set about finding a means of communicating the merger to both businesses which would have credibility, would douse the most misleading rumours and would create positive attitudes. They did not want however to pre-empt any measures in the as yet unformed package of detailed actions which they now wanted the companies themselves to work out. They wanted to be straight and positive.

The meetings very quickly saw the need to invite the 'invisible team' of senior management from NB and CIS into the decision making process for it was they who would bear the brunt of the implementation. There were signs of growing resentment amongst the group at being kept in the dark.

Another feature of the meetings, was to help the steering group to articulate more clearly what they knew and understood and what they didn't know and needed to work on or get help on in making the merger come to life.

They subsequently agreed measures for bringing in the senior management group from NB and CIS. The aim was to secure their commitment by sub-contracting as much as possible of the detailed pre-merger planning to them, especially on the question of whether the change should happen all at once or be paced over a longer period.

First one-day launching conference

The formal announcement of the merger was made at a one-day conference attended by the whole steering group, and forty-five senior managers from both companies.

As consultants we had designed the format of the day and were present to guide and advise the Steering Group as it unfolded. The first purpose of the day, apart from the formal announcement, was to create full and common understanding amongst the senior group of the vision behind the merger and to provide ample opportunities for clarification. The second purpose was to enable managers from the two companies to get to know each other and to understand more about each company. The third purpose was to enable the group to get to know us, the consultants. And finally, considerable time was spent involving the group in a preliminary diagnosis of the major issues that would need solving if the implementation was to be smooth and successful. We were also able to outline the proposed next steps in the implementation process.

Meetings with senior NB and CIS staff

These happened very quickly after the senior staff group had received formal confirmation that the merger was to happen. Our role as neutral outsiders was to talk confidentially to each member of this senior group in order to put together a picture of each company's perceptions of its strengths, what it could uniquely offer the merger and what it could potentially gain from the other. Our job was also to clarify each team's perceptions of the other's strengths and weaknesses. We knew from past experience that each team's perceptions of the weaknesses of the other were very likely to be a distortion of the facts, especially where limited competition had existed between the two. There was a danger of these negative views hardening as the stakes got bigger. In our independent role, it was easier for us to introduce more objectivity into the analysis, and to help others sort fact from fiction.

Merger workshops

A series of three merger workshops was held involving the steering group and the forty-five senior managers from both companies. Each workshop had fifteen participants, bringing together carefully mixed groups from each company who were likely to have to work together. On each occasion the steering group attended for the whole of the third and last day. The purpose of each workshop was to develop team-working across the two businesses and to develop more detailed implementation plans for various aspects of the merger.

The first step was for each company group to share its perceptions, both of itself and of the other group, with the others. The aim was to identify sources of potential conflict and misunderstanding which might consume some of the energy which would be needed for the merger itself. A more positive contribution would come from putting the record straight and using the data as an audit of combined strengths. These could then be built on in order to arrive at a consensus on areas where difficulties were more likely to occur. A further expectation was that this phase would contribute significantly to the development of an alternative, shared co-operative culture and to the 'planning the how' of the teams strategy for implementing the merger.

Other aspects of these workshops included:

- Sub-groups contributing to the merger by working on particular operational areas of concern. Comprehensive proposals for action were presented to the steering group on the third day.
- To agree some lines of communication with the steering group and particularly to obtain their commitment to regular two way dialogue. They in turn were concerned to define an early warning system to pick up anything likely to threaten the merger process as it evolved.
- Feeding back to the steering group a series of ideas to refine their vision of Natcom Services. The new top team was also able to articulate its success criteria and to clarify its expectation of those present.
- Agreement on specific actions for implementation and to confirm detailed plans concerning what parts of both businesses would be brought together first.

Second one-day launching conference

The whole senior group and steering group came together once more, this time together with the Main Board of the group. The purpose was to explain the Big Picture and the detailed implementation proposals which had been developed during the three workshops.

At the end of the day every person present was clear about the next steps, key milestones and their own personal role and contribution in the process.

The merger continued at lower levels, still supervised overall by the steering group but largely driven by the senior group who were now committed to its success. There was a widespread feeling that the investment of time and money in planning the how had accelerated the process markedly and that it had contributed to getting the new company working more efficiently and more quickly than was ever thought possible, given the initial suspicion and hostility between the two parties.

COMMENTARY

In our experience joint ventures and mergers often represent the most emotionally charged of organisational situations. The different parties have frequently spent years in antagonistic relationships as competitors. The negative stereotypes generated by this sort of history are compounded where national pride, cultural differences and organisational ethos also intrude.

Little wonder therefore that the creation of Natcom Services aroused powerful feelings, many of them destructive. The welding together of a new team in these circumstances is a daunting task.

The role of external teamworking consultants can be especially valuable in these situations. Their job is to create situations for the controlled release of negative feelings and stereotypes, and their gradual replacement by perceptions based on fact and the analysis of problems based on co-operation and objectivity rather than blame and prejudice. Their role as honest brokers between the different parties is also useful.

The other powerful unifying force in these situations is the articulation of a shared or common vision that transcends the sectional interests of the different parties. Again the consultants' role can be crucial in helping to bring this about.

We regard working with joint ventures and mergers as one of the most challenging of all teamworking assignments. Little has been done in this area, but judging by the high failure rate, there is much to be done if the ideals behind these co-operative ventures are to be realised. Parties embarking on joint ventures or mergers need to give much more serious thought to developing teamworking right from the earliest stages of planning well before antagonism has become too deep rooted to be reversed.

15 Projects within organisations

THE PROBLEM

Radbridge is a well known University in England, with a large sprawling campus spread around the centre of a provincial town. The organisation needed a new telephone exchange because British Telecom, the UK telecommunications agency, had indicated that they were no longer prepared to continue to maintain the existing system because of its age. The decision to purchase and install a new system was made by the Board of Management.

The management of the site, and all site services, was the responsibility of the Development and Estates Officer. Reporting to him were a variety of specialist line managers (for example an Estates Engineer, Security Officer, and Transport Manager). One of these managers was the Telephone Manager. The Development and Estates Officer had complete autonomy in the management of the services, subject to over-riding budget constraints set by the Board of Management.

As soon as it became clear that a new system was needed, the Telephone Manager interviewed key users in the organisation, such as the switchboard operators and secretaries. It soon became apparent that ease and simplicity of use was their main requirement. He then prepared a report on the size and outline specification of a new system.

Based on existing data the initial report suggested a new electronic exchange with one hundred exchange lines and one thousand extensions, with capacity for a further five hundred extensions, in addition to a number of time saving and cost monitoring facilities.

With the aid of this preliminary data the Development and Estates officer and Telephone Manager contacted various suppliers of large systems, and arranged to meet sales teams from each. Through them, visits were also made to customers of their systems.

Within a month, the Development and Estates Officer and the Telephone Manager had a reasonable knowledge of what systems were on the market, their capability, and their approximate cost.

Arising from this survey the Development and Estates Officer reported to the Board of Management on the need for a new system, and the estimated cost. His report also suggested ways of financing the purchase which had been a preoccupation of the Board. Following this report, the Board of Management agreed in principle to proceed and authorised the Development and Estates Officer to obtain tenders for the new system, and report back in due course.

The Development and Estates Officer then prepared a tender document. This was based on knowledge of Radbridge's current system, taking into account new developments. The tender also drew heavily on the experiences of other users of the various systems, who had been visited during the preliminary stages.

At the same time the Development and Estates Officer considered, with the Estates Engineer, the most appropriate location for the new exchange room. The existing exchange room occupied prime space in the principal administrative building on the site. It was therefore agreed to construct an extension to an outlying building for the new exchange. Accordingly the Estates Engineer, under the guidance of the Development and Estates Officer, instructed an Architect to prepare a scheme and seek tenders. The new exchange room was required to conform to British Telecom standards.

Tenders for the new system and the exchange room were obtained. Following detailed analysis of all the figures, and confirmation from British Telecom that the specifications for both the system and the exchange room were acceptable, a full report was submitted to the Board of Management by the Development and Estates Officer. This included detailed proposals about how the project was to be financed as well as the answer to a number of the concerns that they had expressed as the project unfolded. Approval to proceed was given with a target completion date sixteen months later, to coincide with the opening of a new building on the campus.

THE APPROACH

Following signature of the various contracts the Development and Estates Officer brought together a Project Team consisting of the Telephone Manager, the Estates Engineer, the Architect, representatives of the system supplier and representatives of British Telecom (who in addition to approving the technical specification, were to rewire the site).

The project team met regularly throughout the next twelve months. The team acted as a steering group and the point of communication on all technical and timescale matters, although detailed bilateral discussions also took place between the different parties. No financial matters were discussed in the project team, since there were individual agreements between the various supplier organisations (the building contractor, the system supplier and British Telecom/Radbridge). Any financial discussions were therefore handled direct between the supplier organisations and the Development and Estates Officer.

At the same time the organisation and users were told regularly what was being done, culminating in the weeks before start-up with detailed training for all users in how to operate and benefit from the new system.

The project team was therefore a co-ordinating body, although frequently suggestions on how to overcome particular technical problems were made (and accepted) at the meeting. The Development and Estates Officer chaired the team, with the Telephone Manager providing day-to-day operational leadership.

The project was completed on time and within budget. This was despite the fact that some elements were delayed or not up to specification on initial installation. These problems were overcome largely because they could be anticipated, discussed, aired and resolved within the project team without requiring any subsequent discussions. Since the project team had a flexible membership, and the various supplier organisations sent the most appropriate representative to each meeting, depending on the aspects to be discussed, lines of communication within their organisations were short, with the result that action was fast.

COMMENTARY

This short case study is a classic example of making the invisible team visible. By bringing together all those who had a stake in its success, both insiders and outsiders, the project was tightly co-ordinated with a true sense of common purpose.

It also demonstrated the different success criteria that the Development and Estates Officer had to integrate. On the one hand his sponsors were concerned with cost, method of financing and subsequently timing. British Telecom and Radbridge itself set both hard criteria in the form of technical standards. In addition the users of the system had set soft criteria (ease and simplicity of use).

The important contribution of other resources outside the organisation is also highlighted in the form of other system users, whose experience was invaluable in assessing what was wanted and who was best to supply it. Another feature too is the role of the Management Board as sponsors, who made their criteria and parameters clear, leaving the team leader to get on with the job, but ensuring that they and the rest of the organisation were regularly updated.

Many such in-company projects do not go so smoothly because not enough thought is given to the teamworking that is needed for success.

16 Teamworking across departments

Logicorp manufactures, installs and services highly sophisticated electronic surveillance equipment. They had grown successfully over ten years, but anticipated some new problems unless they took action.

THE PROBLEM

How to deal with the consequences of rapid growth

After ten very innovative and successful years on one site Logicorp had grown steadily to one thousand employees. Through acquisition, and the opening of overseas subsidiaries their size doubled in one year to a World turnover of $140 million. Projections were for one hundred per cent growth in each of the subsequent two years and operations on at least ten sites in five continents.

How to preserve what's best

The company was adamant that certain important elements of its past success must not be lost if they grew bigger. These were

- Identification of individuals with the company's success.
- Informal cross-departmental communication, teamworking and flexibility.
- An attitude that fostered change and innovation.

How to integrate new people quickly

New people were coming into the organisation in large numbers and at all levels through recruitment and acquisition. The problem was how to help them to operate effectively within the company as quickly as possible.

Rapid growth also brought rapid promotions with the result that teams were forever changing their members with consequent effects on the team's performance.

How to develop management capability in parallel with growth

The average age of company employees was thirty. Many people had progressed rapidly and held considerable managerial responsibility at an early age. There was an urgent need to accelerate and broaden the experience of the senior levels of management, particularly those who would be taking up important roles spearheading the next phase of growth.

'In sum,' said the Chief Executive, 'how can we build the team within the organisation by breaking down barriers between functions and helping each other to solve each other's problems?'

THE APPROACH

The Board recognised that the company's success has been built on the very considerable commitment and skill of individual employees and the way they worked together when the company was small.

It also became obvious that these people factors were the key to sustaining success through growth. So they decided to invest heavily in a development programme for their people and through that process to contribute to the continuing development and success of the organisation itself. During the first three years of the programme they involved some hundred and ten managers at a cost in the region of $350,000.

Bringing people together

One element of the strategy was to provide occasions when individuals from all the different parts of the company were brought together informally. A series of one-week courses was run away from the workplace in a residential management centre. Participants were carefully selected from across departments. The course was specially designed to develop new and constructive working relationships between the individuals and to enhance their understanding of other departments roles and contributions. These courses assumed a special importance when it came to integrating people from a recently acquired company.

Focus on teamworking

In parallel with this activity and in conjunction with external consultants the Board highlighted three aspects of teamworking that were particularly important to the future of the company. These were

1. Increasing importance of teamworking *within* departments as they grew bigger.
2. Increasing attention to interdepartmental co-operation and communication as the number of people, buildings, sites, products and markets increased.
3. Increasing need for the Board to delegate to second and third tier management aspects of the development of the business as the Board's scope and role enlarged.

In order to improve the second and third aspects of teamworking as the organisation grew, the Board decided to create some new kinds of formal teams involving the managers who had been on the first series of courses.

Developing teams

The two new kinds of teams were

1. Interdepartmental teams working on current operational problems that spanned departments.
2. Task forces to work on strategic, policy and organisational issues affecting the future development of the company.

A second series of courses was commissioned to enhance these two specific aspects of teamworking. New mixed groups were formed from people who had been on the first course and who again went away for a week.

In addition, and in parallel with these courses, the consultants started to work within the company with two specific departmental teams that were experiencing particular problems. The purpose was to help them improve performance under conditions of constant growth and change.

Fusing learning and action

The second series of courses was designed with two objectives in mind. Roughly half the week was spent in improving core teamworking skills using the Ashridge Team-Working Approach. This included the participants' role as leaders and developers of their own teams. In addition the course members were formed into two new task forces and worked together with consultants over the week to develop themselves into an effective working unit. The Managing Director visited the course with other Board Members to demonstrate the importance that the company attached to the whole people and organisation development programme, to explain the role of inter-departmental teams and task forces, and to act as sponsor for each new task force. During the remainder of the course the task forces spent time 'planning the what and the how' with help from the consultants.

Task forces at work

The task forces then carried out their briefs back in the company, in addition to their normal jobs, usually over a three to six month period.
In most cases the task forces worked through four main stages.

- Negotiating success criteria with the sponsor
- Exploring the problem and finding innovative solutions
- Reporting to and winning the Board's commitment
- Setting up the programme for implementation with those involved, gaining commitment and in many cases managing and monitoring the actual implementation process.

Some of the topics given to the task forces by the Board of Logicorp were:

1. What new businesses should the company be in in seven to ten years time in order to grow to one hundred times its current size?
2. How should the company be structured and managed in order to sustain innovation and motivation as it grows?
3. What will be the information needs of the Board in the next five years and how can they best be met?
4. How can we improve the quality of service to our customers and sustain it as we grow?

COMMENTARY

As with some of the other teamworking projects that we describe, the Logicorp experience demonstrates a number of themes and issues that are being pursued simultaneously.

The central thread in this example is of course the organisation's recognition that, as it grew, and inevitably became more compartmentalised, it had to preserve the climate of informal cross-departmental co-operation that had grown up in its early years. The reason for this was that the organisation understood the direct and well-established connection between teamwork and innovation. Furthermore it realised that this form of teamwork and coordination would become even more important to its future success as the complexity of its business and organisation grew from few products and markets to many and from few locations to many dispersed throughout the world.

Teamworking across departments does not take place without a complex network of contacts and relationships being built up. Many of these contacts of course happen naturally, but in situations of rapid growth and pressure on individuals, the organisation itself can intervene more directly to act as a catalyst in bringing people together. Doing this away from the work situation accelerates and deepens the process.

Another important thread in this instance was the provision of a common strategy and language in the form of the Ashridge Team-Working Approach, to discuss and improve teamworking across departments. A common approach of this nature helps people to see and evaluate what they have to *do*, to make the co-operation and teamworking a reality.

Finally, the Logicorp experience demonstrates once again that most teamwork projects touch all aspects of the organisation's functioning. They are not isolated events that happen on the periphery. They are central to the development of the organisation and its people and as such must have the active sponsorship of senior management. In this instance the whole board of directors was closely involved on a continuing basis, seeing the project as one important part of their responsibility for the strategy and future of the organisation.

17 Enhancing a single team's performance

Springkleen is a manufacturer and distributor of household products that are supplied to ironmongers, supermarkets and department stores. Springkleen is a trading division of a large multinational company. It distributes its products primarily to the UK market under several brand names but also sells internationally through divisions in other countries.

THE PROBLEM

How to make a new structure work smoothly

Over the previous two years the Board of Directors of Springkleen had evolved a new structure. On the one hand were four separate "business centres", semi-autonomous units each manufacturing and marketing different products. On the other hand were four central service functions, finance, personnel, distribution and sales, the latter two operating a fleet of lorries and a sales force that serviced all four business centres. In parallel with this Springkleen had recently incorporated a smaller division of the parent company which formed a new fifth business centre. This kind of structure is sometimes known as a matrix structure.

As a result of these changes, the top team expanded from six to ten members. Five of the original six, who had created the new structure, were members of the expanded team. In addition each business unit was now run by a new general management team consisting of a Chief Executive and specialists who had been allocated from disbanded central functional departments previously looking after all products.

How to address issues within the team

The Chief Executive and Personnel Director of Springkleen had immediately identified the need to weld the extended team together. Subsequently they wanted to focus on the new teams in the business centres.

In talking to all the members of the top team a number of themes began to emerge which were holding back their ability to perform.

- Failure to integrate new members and make them feel part of the expanded team
- The size of the team (ten) making discussion and decision making difficult.
- Poor strategic thinking — some individuals with no experience of looking across divisions and a tendency to spend too much time on operational detail.
- Difficulty in identifying where the common interest and purpose of the team lay, and how best to use the different individuals' talents.
- Inadequately structured and controlled meetings, bogged down by excessive paperwork.

How to resolve outstanding business issues

There also emerged some urgent business issues facing the team which had not yet been fully debated and resolved. The most central was that there were widely differing views about the Division's strategic role and future contribution to the parent. There was also a widespread desire to go back to basics by examining the role of the top team in managing the new structure. Part of this was to redefine the power distribution, relationships and interfaces between the two sides of the matrix, the business centres and the specialist services. Another aspect was how to manage the trade-offs that had to be made say in capital investment, or national advertising between different business centres or brands.

These then were the issues that were preoccupying the leader and members of this newly formed top team. Our role was to help them to resolve these speedily and constructively so that they could then move the division forward.

THE APPROACH

Diagnosis and developing commitment

- In-depth confidential interviews with each member of the Board exploring their view of the Board's functioning.
- Similar interviews with selected individuals within the division who had significant involvement with the Board's proceedings and decisions.
- A report summarising the Board's strengths and potential, while highlighting unresolved teamworking and business issues.
- Further discussions with the Managing Director and Personnel Director about

  - the most practical and effective way to accelerate the team's development
  - how to ensure the full commitment of all Board members to the development process.

Finding ways forward

- Final agreement on a two-and-a-half day Board Performance Workshop away from the office.
- A design for the workshop which included the following elements.

  - An address by the Managing Director on the Boards success criteria and the Division's role within the wider business.
  - Short lectures on approaches to strategy formulation
  - Periods to work on major issues, specifically 'The role of the

Board' and 'The Integration of the fifth Business Centre' into the Division.
- Observations and feedback from consultants and joint planning of clear strategies for performance improvement.
- Questionnaires to highlight the range of membership skills and attitudes within the team.

Making it stick

- A range of decisions and specific action points both on teamworking and business issues followed the workshop.
- An agreed implementation plan for these decisions and a process whereby the team reviewed and monitored its own progress.
- Individual counselling of Board members after the workshop to set personal improvement goals.
- Declaration of these to the whole Board — pairs of Board members meet regularly to review.
- Periodic attendance by consultants at Board and strategy meetings to review and reinforce important aspects of the team's functioning.
- Consultants subsequently working with selected board members and their own Business Centre or Service teams.

COMMENTARY

For any team, the decision to subject itself to scrutiny is no easy one, even more so when the team is at a crossroads. This was particularly so for the Board of Springkleen, recently expanded to ten, facing new challenges in the market place and putting into practice a complex new organisational structure.

It is often at times like these that enlightened teams see the need for some short-term outside support. Less mature teams tend to deny the need, or see asking for help as an admission of failure or a diversion away from 'real work' when they can ill afford the time. Not so. This teamworking project illustrates clearly how the whole of the Springkleen Board development programme was *real work* on the real business issues they faced. Indeed we would go further and say that one of its key outcomes was to help the Board define more clearly what their 'real work' really was.

The primary purpose of a team development programme such as

that at Springkleen is to accelerate natural processes of performance improvement and to set higher standards. This applies equally to the development of individuals who, in this programme, learned a great deal about themselves as well as about their colleagues. The care and sensitivity with which consultants work with individuals within the team, should be just as important a criterion for their selection to do a programme of this nature as their expertise in the functioning of teams.

There are three classic phases to a team development programme such as this. The first is joint diagnosis by consultants and team members of the problems and opportunities (both the 'what' and the 'how') facing the team. This is also an important phase for establishing credibility and trust between consultants and team. The second phase is the development activity itself where work issues are addressed and used as the vehicle for examining how the team is functioning. The result of this phase is a blueprint for subsequent action, the implementation, reinforcement and monitoring of which is the function of the third phase.

Reinforcement can also come by recognising that all team members in this instance are leaders of their own teams one level down. Similar team development programmes cascading down to this second level reinforce common groundrules as well as providing the opportunity to examine the nature of the teamworking relationship between the Board and the second level teams.

18 Developing team leaders and project managers

RDL International is a highly respected R & D organisation with a world wide reputation built on its success in trouble shooting, largely for the motor industry. Organisationally it has a long-standing tradition of specialisation, with departments representing major areas of the company's activities. These include a research laboratory, test facility, design department and development engineering. Project responsibility shifts through the departments as the weight of activity changes. Co-ordination comes from formal links at senior level between the groups in the form of regular project review meetings.

But change is in the air. Client demands have been increasing in complexity with added pressure for shorter delivery times. RDL has been accustomed to a fairly leisurely lifestyle, relying heavily on its reputation to impress the client. A much bigger threat though comes from two competitors, one based in Germany and the other in Italy. Both have gained significant business in what had been a virtual monopoly for RDL.

The top management held extensive discussions to identify ways of revitalising RDL and regaining its position of strength. Their conclusion was that they needed to develop the organisation into a more responsive form which could mobilise its significant talent dramatically better than at present. Their aspiration was for an organisational system which supported the rapid grouping and re-grouping of multi-disciplinary project teams, each sufficiently talented and self-sufficient to be able to achieve a high level of success. They saw these teams supported by an infrastructure of services in such a way that they would cut out current bureaucratic procedures, be able and prepared to second members into the project teams full time so as to give all their energies to the task, and move in rapidly with extra specialist support for the teams where necessary.

A Director of the company was given the brief to develop this broad vision into a comprehensive and detailed proposal. He was able to identify one main obstacle to success. In the past, professional dedication to engineering and research excellence had created serious flaws in RDL's management structure. Many of the company's managers saw themselves as unwilling victims of a reward system which tended to promote the best technical staff into line-management roles. By and large they were unskilled and lacked sophistication in management practices and behaviour. The dominant attitude was one which devalued management, and particularly people and financial management. Many of the line managers waited eagerly for their next opportunity of getting involved closely with a technical problem. To develop a new approach, in which not just managerial, but leadership skills were at the core, would demand a radical re-adjustment of attitudes and new kinds of role.

THE PROBLEM

• **How do you influence potential team leaders to accept a fundamentally new role and to be willing to develop the skills, attitudes and behaviour which would be the essential building blocks of its success?**
• **How do you help them to come to terms with losing direct control over their first love — engineering?**
• **And how do you get there with genuine commitment rather than through coercion?**

The challenge to developing team leaders in this context threw up some quite distinctive issues:

Multi-disciplines

To provide each team with broad technical self-sufficiency would mean integrating members from many different disciplines in the applied sciences. On the one hand this might effectively block any enthusiasm and natural inclination on the leaders part to get too involved. He or she simply wouldn't possess the range of in-depth competences to do so confidently. On the other, it would make unfamiliar demands on the leaders ability. The leader would have to generate and maintain a sense of unity of purpose and shared interest in success among a group of people who each saw different sets of priorities from their own professional view points.

The problem therefore was how to communicate to team leaders a redefined role which places a premium on social, interpersonal, managerial skills and in such a way that they 'buy' it.

Shifting membership

Membership stability for some projects would be low. This would often happen because a project would create demands for a front-end loading of key specialists whose role would reduce as the project moved on. There would then be a build-up of new expertise to take the project forward. Significant shifts in membership might be expected two or three times in the life of a project. In addition other members would be needed for frequent short stays in teams before moving on to service other teams.

How then to develop the leader's skills in bringing new people on board with a project quickly, getting them accepted and fully integrated into the team. How also to deal with short-stay members who might not fit the success culture that the core team had developed.

Projects started immediately by the new teams would tend to be short term (6–9 months) since they represented the organisation's fast-response mechanism in meeting urgent client demands. How then to get short-life teams working very well very quickly in order to regain client confidence?

Overdone analysis

Team leaders, in common with team members in this organisation, were prone to analysing problems to death. They also tended to be intolerant of uncertainty which could not be reduced through hard data. The result was that they were slow to act or react until they felt they had all the facts — which was sometimes never, in the more complex projects. The result was that they were often seen as both rigid and indecisive.

How then to replace a culture characterised by analysis and objectivity, with one which gave priority to action as the basis for dealing with situations. Specifically there was a need to strengthen the leaders' ability to be flexible as well as to be decisive and single minded, to be tough and analytical, as well as supportive and encouraging to team members.

Finding the right words

A language for communicating about team-working and human resource management issues was missing from the experience of leaders and members. Without a language, there were equally few concepts about effective teamworking. 'Planning-the-how' would at best be trivialised unless leaders could articulate clearly and comprehensively what sorts of teams they needed to create.

Hierarchy

A strong sense of order and hierarchy pervaded the organisation. Authority was vested in managers in a formal structure that fixed relationships and either sanctioned individuals to act in limited areas or prevented them. Team leaders had been matured in this environment.

Yet the spirit of the new teams was to be one of single-minded pursuit of outstanding results without letting anything (including the rest of the organisation) stand in the way.

How then to develop in leaders the confidence to challenge the unacceptable, and to cross old authority boundaries. And how too to get the rest of the organisation to adapt itself in order to provide the right environment within which the teams could be successful.

THE APPROACH

Sponsoring

Legitimising the new values and aspirations behind the teams was clearly the responsibility of senior management. The first part of the plan involved working closely with the Research Director, who became the sponsor of the new approach. The process involved helping him to articulate the vision, to identify the payoffs for individuals and the organisation and to see the link between specific new leadership approaches and the achievement of the new way of working. It also involved helping him to put his ideas over in a rather more inspiring way. He was intellectually excited by the vision but had a tendency to sound bored by what he was saying, which did not have the desired inspirational effect on others!

All team leaders and department heads were brought together for a presentation by the Research Director. In establishing the vision he also signalled the organisation's commitment to the process. He also acknowledged that senior management would find it difficult to 'let go' of authority and would be dependent on help and understanding from team leaders in making the transition.

Developing new skills

A one-week residential workshop brought together eight newly appointed team leaders as well as the first of the new teams. This team was to be together for six months, working on a priority project which had some major problems. The workshop was dedicated to:

- Developing basic team-leading skills, using exercises specifically designed to give controlled learning opportunities in a 'safe' environment. Emphasis was given to colleague feedback on the grounds that the acquisition of feedback skills would make a significant impact on understanding the notion of leadership in a team environment.
- Insight into personal leadership style. Questionnaires were used to give leaders information about themselves as well as a language to talk about leadership concepts and practices. This combined with the Ashridge Team-Working Approach, provided a new way of talking about performance and teamworking.
- The eight new leaders established their own blueprint on leadership practices, building on the experience of the working team and drawing on a growing understanding of the role of the leader in team development.
- Negotiations on success criteria with senior management emphasised areas in which tangible support would be needed both for team leaders and for senior management. In effect each went through a process of re-negotiating contracts with the other, establishing expectations about specific changes in management

attitudes and practices to support the move toward a more open, candid and risk-taking style of leadership.

- The new team was tasked with putting together a blue-print for summarising how it needed to work in order to achieve its mission. Much of what they did was filmed on video, with the other eight leaders as observers. The leader of the working team as well as its members were given feedback from colleagues, other team leaders and the consultants on how to improve their performance. Observing this provided valuable learning for the eight team leaders.

Implementation

Two company trainers worked alongside the consultants at all stages of the process. With the development of commitment to the implementation of the blueprints from senior management, the new team, and the eight team leaders, the company went ahead with the process, using their two internal trainers to take subsequent teams through similar but adapted development activities.

Similar programmes have been run with organisations wanting to develop the skills of project managers running teams of various kinds within the organisation. For instance, one company had project managers co-ordinating the building of new High Street stores, and another had project managers who ran new product development teams. In this latter case, the consultants who ran the programme went in-company with some of the project managers to help them apply the lesson of the programme to developing their own teams. This involved working a day a month over six months with the whole team together.

COMMENTARY

In the changing future of organisations that we outline earlier in the book, the role of the team leader or project manager of a multidisciplinary team will become more widespread. The contribution of these roles to the success of the organisation will also become more important.

RDL recognised it had a problem shared by many organisations. The role is very different from that of either line management or technical specialists. It is probably more demanding than both and certainly more stressful. And there is a scarcity of people available with the all round capabilities required.

The only answer, as RDL found, is to invest in accelerating the development of such people through providing opportunity, training and support for those with the motivation and potential. Investing in this particular cadre of people, who above anyone else influence the workings of teams within the organisation, is a relatively low-cost approach designed to groom the few in order to influence the behaviour of the many. If this initial preparation and development of the leaders can then be cascaded down to helping them with the development of their whole teams, then the chances of more lasting success are enhanced.

There are distinct advantages to an organisation that is large enough to have sufficient leaders to justify developing programmes tailored to their specific needs. They are able to develop and work within a teamworking framework that fits the particular style and situation of the organisation. Smaller organisations, with fewer team leaders, may create special development programmes for individuals in conjunction with teamworking consultants or rely on the range of programmes offered by management colleges and training organisations.

Some guidelines for success

'Can you guarantee this teamworking project will work?' asked a rather apprehensive Personnel Manager. 'No', said one of us, 'but we have some good ideas about what needs to happen to give it the best chance of success'. In the end we didn't go ahead with this particular organisation because it soon became clear that the conditions were not right; neither the organisation nor the teams in question had the will to make it work.

In all the teamworking projects outlined in the preceding chapters there are three main parties involved in successful implementation. There is the management itself, the team or teams, and the internal or external teamworking consultant. In this final chapter we want to summarise the role of each of these three parties and provide some guidelines for each that have emerged out of our own, and other people's work.

THE MANAGEMENT'S ROLE

In practice what we refer to as the management's role is usually that of the senior management or management two levels above that of the team members. For it is they who will need to provide the initiative and take the responsibility for improving teamworking within the

172

organisation. It is they above any of the other parties who can create the right conditions. If the senior management really want it to succeed and are excited about what it can achieve, then success is already half way to being achieved.

This is not to say that they are the only important ones. The attitudes of the sponsor (if different from senior management) and the service departments are crucial too. A key service department head in one of our client firms held a whole teamworking project to ransom for six months through his belligerent refusal to co-operate.

What then are some of the organisational factors that can tip a teamworking project towards success or failure? We hope the following comments provide some guidelines for management.

1 *Don't engage in too much detailed planning at senior level before involving the team(s)*

Part of the secret of getting the team committed and excited is to decentralise a lot of the planning to them. Because they are on the ground they will do it better. You stick to providing the vision and the Big Picture. If you have done too much planning be prepared to let go of it. They will probably do it better.

2 *Be prepared to divest responsibility and authority to Superteams*

If you provide an exciting vision, assemble them, train them and then *trust* them, they will surely achieve significant results. Superteams will want to exercise initiative and authority in order to get things done. This does not mean that you lose your authority.

3 *Be prepared to be open to the Superteam's ideas*

They will become very authoritative, and will know more than you. If you respect them and learn from them, they and the organisation will benefit hugely. If you are threatened by or are antagonistic towards their confidence, neither of you will benefit.

4   Be prepared for some feelings of anxiety or discomfort

After all you won't be totally in control of what they do. But if you have contracted well with them, and given clear direction and parameters, they will be coming to you if they want to go outside those.

5   Don't get cold feet

The worst thing you can do is to put the brakes on as soon as the teams take a few risks, or hit problems, or make apparently slow progress in the early stages. These events need to occur if they are to develop into outstanding performers. You have to let them grow up.

6   Don't shunt responsibility for the project elsewhere

We find a common pattern is that senior management are much in evidence at the interesting time when a teamwork project is being launched. They then hand the whole thing over to some junior training manager and disappear just when the real hard work begins.

Another ploy is to leave it all to the consultants to make the running. We don't allow that to happen. It's *your* programme. Take responsibility for it.

7   Don't just 'play the game' — the teams will find you out

If you make great new demands of your teams but then show by your subsequent behaviour that you want things to stay the same, then you are setting them up for failure. A good team will confront you and either sort it out or pull out of the game. You must ensure that you are all playing to the same teamworking rules.

8   Demonstrate your commitment by removing obstacles

There are sometimes people within the organisation who persist in acts of sabotage against Superteams. These are often individuals who have built up prestige in the organisation as departmental chiefs. We have encountered startling instances of where these people used their reputations to block and to cause great anguish.

Are you prepared to take action with people like this?

9   *If you're not prepared to invest substantial money and people's time in the project, don't start*

Just as in capital investment, under-investment in the human system is often wasted investment. Too often we are confronted with senior decision makers who say, 'can't we get away with just putting a few people through the programme'. All the evidence suggests that, in order to improve teamworking across the organisation, you have to develop a critical mass of people in the organisation all thinking along the same lines to make any real difference. We would suggest five to ten per cent of the managerial population as a rule of thumb and a similar percentage of their salary bill invested in the process, if it is to make any real impact on improving teamworking across the organisation as a whole.

10   *Get the sponsorship right*

Sponsors who believe they can just vote the money and leave it there are a liability. Sponsors must take a visible and active part in promoting and explaining the objectives of teamworking programmes. If they don't believe in it, they shouldn't do it.

Particularly where interdepartmental teams or task forces start working, the sponsor's active role is crucial in clarifying performance expectations and ground rules, in smoothing the way and gaining commitment at the higher levels, and in maintaining a supportive and open minded style. The sponsor whose mind is already made up is not a good example of teamworking.

The role and attitude of the sponsor should never be underestimated. It is the most tangible evidence available to the team of the legitimacy and value of its mission. The sponsor is the most important and powerful agency in selling the team, its methodology and ideals to the rest of the organisation. The sponsor is the guardian of the team's vision, protecting it against predators and maintaining its integrity. It is through the sponsor that the team tests out new ways of handling responsibility, using influence and negotiating success criteria. The unique relationship between team and sponsor also serves as the meeting point at which new understandings are reached between team and organisation.

THE TEAM'S ROLE

The team's role is simple — to demonstrate that it can achieve outstanding results that are valued by its clients, its sponsors, and the wider organisation. And that involves doing what it has to do to become a Superteam.

Apart from this there are some considerations to do with the team or teams, that can help to create the right conditions for success in the early stages of a teamworking project.

1 Publicise the vision and the Big Picture widely

Get as many people as possible within the organisation caught up in the excitement of what you are trying to achieve. If you are doing this together with your sponsors, you can build momentum and support in your favour.

That means you and the sponsor doing a lot of talking often. One task force systematically identified key people who could be affected by their recommendations, took active steps to involve them and sought their opinions and to understand their concerns. They tested out their draft recommendations on them and amended them in the light of some of their comments. The task force was determined to earn their respect and commitment.

We have been impressed by the energy which successful teams put into selling themselves to the rest of the organisation and the effect this has on the development of extensive networks that cut across functional boundaries and in doing so greatly enhances the power of the team to get things done.

2 Try to select the right sort of people for the team

You don't only want members with the right technical abilities — you want people with good teamworking attitudes and skills too. If there is a choice, exercise it. In most of the teams we have experienced, it has been apparent that achieving success is as dependent on the availability of simple interpersonal and influencing skills as it is on the development of technical sophistication.

3 Bring together people from within an organisational unit who have some legitimate reason to work together

One of our clients was a multinational conglomerate that brought together members of teams from different subsidiaries in different businesses in different countries. While they learned a lot for themselves about teamworking, we doubt whether they went back for their companies and single handed improved teamworking or co-operation between subsidiaries.

It is much better to choose people from within the same company, division or site. Its even alright to have people across companies or divisions provided that their roles have some common purpose. One group was keen to pull together all its purchasing managers. An electrical group bidding for major international power projects, brought together a number of groups at different levels across its divisions to co-ordinate the tendering process. The main thing is that teams should have real, important work to do together.

4   Be open to learning from the organisation

It is very tempting when starting off in a new team to want to prove yourselves by doing it all yourselves. Resist the temptation. You gain a lot of respect by asking others what they think, or how they would approach it. There's a lot of talent about — use it first and then build on it with your own.

5   Build support systems

We have come to attach particular significance to the development of support systems. If an organisation is using several Superteams simultaneously, growth can be dramatically speeded up, by setting up groups across teams who can meet regularly in a safe-house to share problems, learn from and support each other and provide support to members who are in trouble. A group consisting of all the team leaders can be particularly valuable, often with a consultant to help them come to terms with their demanding and often stressful roles.

THE CONSULTANT'S ROLE

Organisations that already have highly motivated teams that perform well don't need consultants. But in most cases of teamworking projects, the organisation lacks the experience both of high performing teams, and the introduction of new teamworking strategies.

In these circumstances an internal or external consultant, with the necessary experience and skills, has an important role to play. Consultants will work directly with sponsors, steering groups and teams. They will also need to work with even more senior and service function management. Their first role is to helicopter, reviewing the progress of the entire teamworking project with their client(s) and initiating action as necessary to keep it on track. Their second role is to work on the ground in a training, development or consultancy role with individuals and teams to help them improve their performance.

These are some of the common considerations for consultants managing teamworking projects. They are also important considerations for the client organisation to discuss with the consultants.

1 Try to work with a new team after it has had a few meetings

By this stage the team has begun to settle down, started to look at its task, and has some real issues to work on improving. These tend to be better fodder for development activities than abstract or theoretical notions. We like to start straight off with the team talking about what it has to do to be successful. Personal and interpersonal issues tend to come latter.

2 Get close to the sponsor early

Getting to know the sponsor as a person early on is very important. Sponsorship gets into difficulties if it is diffuse and with no focus. The consultant's role is to help the sponsor clarify and rehearse the role. It works best when the sponsor has real conviction about a better future, is willing to stay loyal to the team and not ditch them when the going gets tough.

On the other hand, the consultant will have to intervene if the sponsor, however committed and enthusiastic, clearly does not have the necessary clout or backing of the organisation. Alternatively, the warning bells will usually start to ring when the sponsor or senior management, despite expressions of commitment, can never be pinned down to a meeting because they are too busy. Their behaviour, in this instance, reveals that their true priority is to be elsewhere.

3 Ensure good team leaders

Teamworking projects are much more likely to succeed, when

leaders who have been chosen for their competence and ability to earn authority and respect. The teams need leaders who can respond adaptively, who can be tough when things begin to fall apart, who can be sustaining when the team is under sustained pressure and who can be analytical and dispassionate when standing back looking at the big picture.

If consultants are not satisfied with the quality of the proposed leaders they should make their views known and influence the selection process.

4   Provide particular support to team leaders

Leading a potential Superteam is a demanding and stressful activity, especially for specialists who have little experience of managing people.

Consultants can be of considerable help to these individuals by talking their roles through with them, monitoring and reviewing progress, and providing coaching. The consultant can also act sometimes as a broker between sponsor, organisation and leader to diagnose problems and initiate solutions. Consultants can also form a number of leaders into a support group where appropriate, as well as working with team members on how they can be of help to the leader.

5   Have regular shorter contacts over a long period rather than a temporary involvement

Teamworking projects are more likely to be successful when consultants are able to work with both team and organisation on a frequent, short in–out basis rather than being expected to complete the work in a single large chunk, with few opportunities to follow through. We would rather spend five times two days running through say the first six months of the teams life rather than ten days at the beginning or at the point where the team has first formed. Our ideal is three phases. The first is short visits for diagnosis. The second is longer contact time to go more deeply into issues, and the third an extended monitoring consisting of short visits, perhaps reinforced from time to time with longer periods of contact.

6   *Take the team's sponsors and other relevant parties away from their working environment for important developmental activities*

Planning the How of good teamworking in organisations takes time. It is difficult to stand back and look dispassionately at the way you work while trying to keep the show on the road. Relationships take time to be formed. A week away or even two-and-a-half days with a team can accelerate all these processes dramatically. Teams whose relationships might take a year to develop under the pressures of daily work, can be made to work better and quicker in a matter of days if they leave their work behind. This is particularly so when new project teams are being formed.

The argument that people are too busy or haven't got enough time is irrelevant. It usually means that no-one is really committed to improving things.

7   *Be prepared to blow the whistle*

Consultants are employed to use their professional experience and judgement in order to help their clients' teamworking projects to succeed. If the consultants find that some of the ground has not been properly prepared, or if insufficient support or investment is forthcoming to make it work, or some major blockages are not being removed, then they must confront those issues with both client and sponsors. The motivation is two-fold. They don't want their clients and all the others in the organisation to waste time, energy and money only to fail or at best achieve mediocre results. Second, they themselves like to be associated not with failure but with success.

Index

Please add the following name to your mailing list.

_____

_____

_____

_____ Zip _____

Primary Organizational Affiliation: [ ] fill in with one number from below

1. Education
2. Business & Industry
3. Religious Organization
4. Government Agency
5. Counseling

6. Mental Health
7. Community, Voluntary, and/or Service Organization
8. Health Care
9. Library
0. Consulting

Please add the following name to your mailing list.

_____

_____

_____

_____ Zip _____

Primary Organizational Affiliation: [ ] fill in with one number from below

1. Education
2. Business & Industry
3. Religious Organization
4. Government Agency
5. Counseling

6. Mental Health
7. Community, Voluntary, and/or Service Organization
8. Health Care
9. Library
0. Consulting

BUSINESS REPLY CARD

FIRST CLASS   PERMIT NO. 11201 SAN DIEGO, CA

POSTAGE WILL BE PAID BY ADDRESSEE

UNIVERSITY ASSOCIATES
Publishers and Consultants
8517 Production Avenue
San Diego, California 92121

NO POSTAGE
NECESSARY
IF MAILED
IN THE
UNITED STATES

BUSINESS REPLY CARD

FIRST CLASS   PERMIT NO. 11201 SAN DIEGO, CA

POSTAGE WILL BE PAID BY ADDRESSEE

UNIVERSITY ASSOCIATES
Publishers and Consultants
8517 Production Avenue
San Diego, California 92121